The Lifelong Learner

by Ronald Gross

Simon and Schuster / New York

2   3   4   5   6   7   8   9   10

Library of Congress Cataloging in Publication Data

Gross, Ronald.
    The lifelong learner.

    Bibliography: p.
    Includes index.
    1. Self-culture. 2. Continuing education.
3. Study, Method of. I. Title.
LC32.G76   374   77–5106
ISBN 0-671-22524-3

Permission to reprint from the following is gratefully acknowledged:
    Autobiography of Malcolm X, by Malcolm X, copyright © 1964 by Alex Haley and Malcolm X., copyright © 1965 by Alex Haley and Betty Shabazz. Reprinted by permission of Grove Press, Inc.
    Coming to My Senses, by John Robben, copyright © 1973 by John Robben. Reprinted by permission of Thomas Y. Crowell Co., Inc.
    Learning Without a Teacher, by Michael Rossman, Fastback #45, Phi Delta Kappa Educational Foundation, copyright © 1973, 1974 by Michael Rossman. Reprinted by permission of Michael Rossman.
    Positive Addiction, by William Glasser, copyright © 1976 by William Glasser, Inc., Joseph P. Glasser, Alice J. Glasser, and Martin H. Glasser. Reprinted by permission of Harper & Row, Publishers, Inc.
    Working and Thinking on the Waterfront, by Eric Hoffer, copyright © 1969 by Eric Hoffer. Reprinted by permission of Harper & Row, Publishers, Inc.
    Material from "The 19-Inch Campus," by Ronald Gross, November 22, 1975, copyright © 1975 by Triangle Publications, Inc. Reprinted by permission of Triangle Publications, Inc.

Acknowledgments

Besides the people and sources mentioned in the text, and the hundreds of lifelong learners throughout the country who have shared their experiences with me, the following have had the most to do with the writing of this book: Alvin Eurich, Helen Baker, Beatrice Gross, Michael Gross, David Hapgood, John Holt, Cyril Houle, Janet Koch, Eda LeShan, Shelley Neiderbach, John Ohliger, Robert Orser, Robert Rainsbury, Jere and Freddie Rowland.

My full collaborator in the final stages of writing was Judith Murphy, surely the best in her field, whatever that is. Frances Shaw edited the resources section masterfully.

To Dan Green I owe particular gratitude for his guidance and patience throughout. Pat Meehan has been a superb editor.

For financial support of research which strengthened the book I must thank The Ford Foundation, the United States Office of Education, and the Council for the Progress of Non-Traditional Study.

For Bea,
lifelong learner *par excellence*

CONTENTS

9

All men, by nature, desire to know.
—ARISTOTLE

Every man is his own Pygmalion, and spends his life fashioning himself. And in fashioning himself, for good or ill, he fashions the human race and its future.
—I. F. STONE

The Lifelong Learner

Chapter 1 / THE LIFELONG LEARNER

> *Every man who rises above the common level
> has received two educations: the first from
> his teachers; the second, more personal and
> important, from himself.*
> —EDWARD GIBBON

You are already something of a lifelong learner, or you wouldn't have started reading this book. In your own way, you may well have done many of the things I will propose. But you also may have felt from time to time that you could learn even more, do it better, and have more fun at it. If so, you are just the kind of reader I am looking for.

Do you recognize in yourself any of these characteristics of lifelong learners?

- You are open to new experiences, ideas, information, and insights. You like to make things happen instead of waiting for life to act on you.
- There are always things you'd love to know more about, appreciate better, or learn to do. In fact, you never have the feeling that you know everything , have every skill, you'll ever need to know.
- You feel better about yourself when you are successfully learning something new.
- You've learned enormously from certain important experiences which don't usually rate as "subjects."
- You often learn a great deal in ways other than taking courses.
- The kind of life you want to lead five years from now requires that you begin to learn new things now.

• You believe that investing in your own growth is the best investment in your future—occupational or personal.
• You have been attracted by, or perhaps are already enrolled in, one of the new kinds of educational programs for adults offered by colleges and universities around the country.

Lifelong learning means self-directed growth. It means understanding yourself and the world. It means acquiring new skills and powers—the only true wealth which you can never lose. It means investment in yourself.

Lifelong learning means the joy of discovering how something really works, the delight of becoming aware of some new beauty in the world, the fun of creating something, alone or with other people.

To become a lifelong learner—or a *better* lifelong learner —is to become more alive. Each day becomes an adventure in discovery, challenging you to add to your experience and knowledge. Rather than a struggle within well-worn ruts, the passing weeks and months become milestones in your constant exploration, inquiry, and development.

To the lifelong learner, a chance acquaintanceship on a plane trip becomes a window into another life-style. A new route to work yields a little lesson in urban planning. A child's unanswerable question sparks a miniature Socratic dialogue. A stimulating television documentary begins a search for answers to a community's problem.

Lifelong learning isn't consciously studying, or having to memorize something someone tells you to, or pursuing a certain set of subjects which schools consider important.

If you are indeed a lifelong learner but haven't ever realized it, that's probably because society has "schooled you up," in Ivan Illich's phrase, so that you equate learning only with what is taught in educational institutions. Many people have trouble at first with the concept of self-directed learning. They can't see that independent, unconstrained, non-institutionalized learning is "real" education. They assume that the "right" way to learn is in a classroom, from a teacher and from texts, through listening to "expert authorities" and doing assigned reading, by taking tests and getting grades.

The lifelong learner is liberated from these superstitions about education—and therefore free to pursue his or her own growth in an infinite variety of ways. So I will often refer to the lifelong learner as a *free learner*. In the rest of this book, lifelong learner and free learner mean the same thing.

Realizing some basic truths about learning and growth can liberate you from overreliance on schooling and strengthen you for the adventure of self-development. These truths— many of them still considered heretical by educators—are that:

1. Adults who take command of their own learning often master more things, and master them better, than those who rely on being taught. They tend to have greater zest, retain more of what they have learned, and make better use of it in their living.
2. Adults learn in different ways than children. We have a different sense of ourselves, of our time, of what's worth learning and why.
3. No one can learn *for* you, any more than a surrogate can love for you or eat for you. "To learn" is an active verb, and you as a learner are unique. Your education is something you must tailor to yourself, not something you can get ready made.
4. No particular way of learning is in itself superior to another. You should design procedures that suit your convenience and taste. How you learn depends on your temperament, circumstances, stage of life, as well as your need, taste, or ambition. Success in learning depends not on the subject itself or the conditions (how, where, when) of learning, but basically on the learner's engagement—his or her fascination and concern for the subject.
5. There is no prescribed curriculum that everybody must or should or can learn in order to be "well educated." In fact, a narrow academic notion of what constitutes education can be a major block to growth. The scope of free learning stretches far beyond the subjects taught in schools and col-

leges. The worth to you of any particular subject or field
is for you to decide on your own terms. Virtually every aspect
of your life—work, leisure, personal relationships, community
activities—has the latent power to enhance your "second education," if you can find or create the ways to learn it.

6. The prime time to learn is when your own need, curiosity,
taste, or hunger impels you in a particular direction. The rule
holds for adults in their developing interests and capacities
as it does for children's miraculous learning to walk and talk.
It's as true for metaphysics or Chaucer as it is for typing or
bridge or bookbinding.

7. Growing older may change what, why, and how you learn,
but it does not diminish your capacity to learn. In fact, provided you've kept your mind and senses busy and alert, it is
demonstrably true that the ability to think and reason often
increases with age.

8. Immersing yourself in a new situation can be a prime way
to learn. A familiar example of this principle is the ease and
speed with which people learn French, say, when constantly
exposed to the language in a French-speaking country. The
principle applies, if less dramatically, to your capacity to
learn from the environments of your daily life. Often people
find that their most effective acquisition of knowledge, skill,
or understanding comes either as the by-product of work or
as a spin-off from something taken up as a diversion.

9. In devising your own curriculum, you can tap an extraordinary array of resources at home, at work, and in the community. You may want to avail yourself from time to time
of the conventional institutions of education, but never under-
estimate the "Invisible University" that exists in our society.
One of the chief purposes of this book is to help you discover
the countless elements of that university, to enable you to
draw on the richness it places at your disposal.

As the opening chapters of this book will reveal, many
adults take charge of their own "second education," learning a formidable range of subject matter and skills, both by
themselves and with others. The ways and reasons are as

various as the learners. (Chapter 5 points out the principal resources available to the free learner. They are legion, and increasing.)

Many ventures into self-education are limited in scope—learning enough Spanish to enhance a trip to Mexico, perhaps, or enough about wiring and plumbing to be your own handyperson. Much of this learning is unself-conscious, an integral part of life, like child care and budgeting and politics or perhaps dancing. Some of it is undertaken for the pure pleasure of stretching the mind—delving into the French Revolution, for instance, or the architecture of the Renaissance.

Some people, by temperament or circumstance attuned to organized goal-directed action, deliberately plan a course of study or even a whole curriculum. These are the exceptions, proving, if you like, the unlimited possibilities of self-teaching. From such examples we might deduce that free learners constitute an elite, a choice group of individualists with the special talent, intelligence, and drive to be their own teachers.

True, the ranks of free learners *are* adorned by outstanding people. Just a few who have succeeded without the "advantage" of a college education are crusading journalist I. F. Stone; inventors Edward Land (the Polaroid camera) and Bill Lear (Lear Jet); anthropologist Richard Leakey; *Cosmopolitan* editor Helen Gurley Brown; social critic Eric Hoffer; and sports promoter Don King. Perhaps the most renowned such case in our time was Winston Churchill, who said, "I have no technical and no university education, and have just had to pick up a few things as I went along." Virtually all successful writers, notwithstanding all the creative writing courses and summer writing workshops, finally learn to write only by writing and by reading.

Other notable contemporaries who received the fullest possible formal education, nevertheless proudly declare themselves to be essentially self-taught. "I am a stubborn little auto-didact," said author and Ph.D. holder Paul Goodman, adding in explanation, "My own way, or none at all." John Houseman, the distinguished stage and film director, speaks of the "auto-didactical" education he got from endless reading during his lonely travels in the grain business before the Great Depression. He believes that his self-conducted study gave him a better education than any learning he had already gotten from several of Europe's finest universities. Buckminster Fuller holds that "True higher learning is self-administered unlearning of most of what we've been taught in school." Stewart Brand, creator of the best-selling *Whole Earth Catalog*, describes his occupation as "just goin' to school in the world."

From the widest imaginable range of people comes the same basic message. Margaret Mead and Groucho Marx, for example, recall strikingly similar experiences with learning vs. schooling. "My grandmother wanted me to get an education," Dr. Mead reports, "so she kept me out of school." And Groucho remembers that "When my mother heard about me cutting out from school she asked me, 'Don't you want to get an education?' I answered, 'Not if I have to go to school to get it.'"

We all share this capability of being lifelong learners. There are innumerable varieties of self-teaching, and it is already a remarkably widespread habit among American adults.

The most striking generalization about free learners is that there is no generalizable pattern to self-education. There has been little rigorous study of the process and its practitioners. Despite its pervasiveness free learning has until recently escaped the notice of educational researchers. Only now are they catching up with the burgeoning of self-education in America and beginning to survey the profusion of knowledge and skills acquired outside of conventional courses in schools and colleges.

No one denigrates the glories of university scholarship at its best or denies the rigorous formal training required to master, say, neurosurgery. There are careers open only to those with the proper credentials. And many people just prefer the ordered pattern of classroom, teacher, semester, course, credit.

Fortunately the do-it-yourself university of free learners is no longer at odds with the billion-dollar bastions of the nation's colleges and universities. New programs, available in every area of the country under such names as "University Without Walls" and "External Degree," offer ways to earn a degree through independent study. These programs eliminate rigid prerequisites and requirements for taking courses, so that you can design your own education around your major concerns, enthusiasms, and work or leisure activities. In such programs sitting in classrooms, taking tests, and piling up credits have been replaced by projects in which you master the skills and acquire the knowledge that you need in the ways that best suit your life-style.

You can even get college credits for what you've already learned on your own. Hundreds of campuses all over the country have issued a standing invitation to free learners to present evidence of their achievements for evaluation for credit. So far the emphasis is on learning that parallels courses or subjects that the institution offers. But the next stage of this process is well in sight, when virtually *any* legitimate learning will be translatable, if the individual wishes, into credits leading to a degree.

In these programs the higher education establishment is making a major accommodation to free learners. Colleges have opened a healthy traffic between the millions who are successfully learning on their own and the campuses with their institutional resources, facilities, and credentialing power.

Whatever path you pick, your "second education" will be personal and individual. It will grow out of your needs, take its shape from your style, and carry you where you choose to go. Perhaps that is the most important thing about free learning—that it affirms and actualizes *you*, a point which has political implications that I will return to at the end of this book.

This idea of self-development is the link between your life and your learning. A free learner seizes the exhilarating responsibility for the growth of his or her own mind. This starts when you realize that you must decide what you will make of yourself. However much your learning and growth involve other people and feed on their insights and skills, in the final analysis it is *you* who must choose and conduct your own process of self-change.

Being a lifelong learner is simply caring consciously—but unsolemnly—about your own self-development. Such caring will quite naturally impel you to use your mind constructively, to relish the challenges to grow which the ever-changing environment presents. "After the needs for food, shelter, and other physical necessities have been met," says educator Jose Orlando Toro, "practically every one of our life-goals involves learning of some kind."

There is a power within each of us to shape and reshape ourselves, in ways large and small, to become more fully what we want to be. Men and women, rich and poor, young and old, have found in this adventure of self-creation some of their deepest pleasures and most life-affirming achievements. Whatever your prior "education," I hope the pages that follow will enliven and strengthen your own lifelong free learning.

Chapter 2 / **LIFELONG LEARNERS IN ACTION**

> *There is a time in every man's education when
> he arrives at the conviction that envy is
> ignorance; that imitation is suicide . . . The
> power which resides in him is new in nature,
> and none but he knows what that is which he
> can do, nor does he know until he has tried.*
> —RALPH WALDO EMERSON

Now I would like you to meet some free learners in action, to see what we can glean from their diverse experiences. Diversity—in purpose, method, scope—is, of course, a prime characteristic of free learning.

The few people you will meet here have been drawn from literally hundreds I've found all over the country over the past several years. Everyone seems to have a favorite example to add—a friend, relative, colleague, or someone he's read about. So I could have picked dozens of others just as interesting and diverse as these free learners. Consider as you meet them, then, that each one stands for a throng of others.

The free learners presented here are, granted, rather special—if only because they have so consciously discerned and expressed what they are up to and where it gets them. But the moral for every practicing or potential free learner is clear: All of these ordinary/extraordinary people taught themselves in ways tailored to their personalities, circumstances, interests, and ambitions.

In making the hard choices for this chapter I deliberately ruled out, with a single exception, famous people and historical figures. The exception is Malcolm X, the assassinated Muslim whose self-education in prison transformed this one-time petty thug into a leader of his people.

Cornelius Hirschberg Learns "The Best That Has Been Thought and Said."

"I am perhaps the first man to put forth for my credentials the fact that I am a man of no special talent or knowledge," Cornelius Hirschberg begins the memoir of his lifelong self-education, *The Priceless Gift* (Simon and Schuster, 1960). "But if I were a professor or a well-schooled writer or a man of high abilities [he was in fact a salesman, now retired], I would not be the kind of man this book is written to help . . . My ways of learning are beyond nobody. I *have* learned more than the average man, and I do live a keener, more enjoyable life than most people seem to, but my results are not beyond them. As I tell the whole story of what I have learned and enjoyed, it will become plain that these pleasures are yours for the taking."

Hirschberg learned that a true liberal education can be achieved in the midst of the busiest adult life. He used the subway ride to and from work each day and his lunch hour. "I have read on subways, trains, and buses for forty years, and on these conveyances, and during my lunchtime, I've done approximately ten hours of reading a week for about two thousand weeks, all of it the most serious reading I do, since I do my light reading at home. Those 20,000 hours add up to at least five college degrees. I got in that much reading during what would have been wasted time which I had to lose and couldn't control in any case. The subway university is one of the best in the world." (Interestingly, Hirschberg's formula for finding the time to learn is very similar to the one Arnold Bennett offered his readers in that classic of years ago, *How to Live on 24 Hours a Day*, which is really a treatise—a delightful one, well worth reading, and recently reissued in paperback—on enlivening your life through free learning.)

Hirschberg lays out "a broad plan that anybody may use, so that you can go to your own university, acquire as much sensitivity and understanding in the arts and sciences as your abilities and leisure permit, learn something of history and literature, and fix the course of your hearing, listening and seeing, once and for all, in a general way, exactly as you would if you matriculated at college. With one difference—this college graduates only when life ends."

Hirschberg's range is astonishing. He offers detailed plans for exploring history, mathematics, the sciences, literature, music, art, and philosophy. At one point he reviews his attempt throughout a decade to pursue a certain line of inquiry:

About ten years ago, I decided that I would settle down to a prolonged reading of philosophy. I decided to read Plato and the other ancients in chronological order, and continue through the years reading at least certain key philosophers, such as Aquinas, Bacon, Spinoza, Leibnitz, Descartes, Locke, Hume, Kant, Hegel, and some moderns. But as soon as I started Plato, I became dissatisfied with my knowledge of Greek history—a discontent which took two years' reading to appease. Such a study of Greek history put me in a state of imbalance with respect to still older history, so reading in Egyptian, Mesopotamian, and Asiatic history became necessary.

I was now forced to consider pre-history. This led to inquiries into the details of the evolution of man, then of animals and plants, and, finally, of the earth itself—a line of reading which would eventually have led me to evaporate into empty space. Fortunately, events made it advisable to refurbish and extend my command of mathematics, which caused several interruptions, adding up to perhaps eighteen months.

What became of philosophy? It is still waiting. Fortunately, those ten years of reading contribute powerfully to the study of philosophy, and if I have a long life, I'll make it yet. I think I can start within two years. . . .

Do I need a doctor? Is a collapse impending? What strains, what tensions! Not at all. This is, was, and always will be fun. I owe this to nobody but myself. I am in no hurry. It will all come out in the wash. If luck is with me, I'll do all that philosophy. I can almost hear metaphysics shiver as I close up on her. And if I don't quite make it, no debts will be left for my heirs to settle. Death quits these claims.

In the eighteen years since *The Priceless Gift* was published, Hirschberg has continued to enliven his life with learning. He closed in on philosophy by bracing himself with several standard texts in mathematical logic, then worked his way through the first fifty-nine theorems of the *Principia Mathematica.* At one point he embarked on the ambitious enterprise of reading through the entire Bible, with diligent attention to commentaries from the linguistic, religious, historical, and anthropological points of view. This scheme made for rewarding reading for several years, until the publisher on whose scholarly edition Hirschberg was depending failed him by discontinuing the series.

In literature, he retraced his steps through the early English poets like Chaucer and Langland, then faced squarely the fact that he had read no great poet outside the English language. "That was no way to go to the grave," he felt. "And since I sought a writer worth years of work, and Goethe can't be appreciated in translation, I was left with Dante." By the age of seventy-five, Hirschberg had happily worked his way (with dictionaries and critiques) through the *Inferno* and the first twenty-two cantos of *Purgatorio.* "A few days ago, I read an entire canto at first sight and got the general meaning right off. Within two years, I should be able to not merely read, but to *feel* Dante."

Summing up these last few years, Hirschberg says, "My personal library has grown to 2500 carefully selected volumes. But my major achievement over the last ten years has been to learn to read them more slowly and to think more deeply as I read. Four pages an hour of something like

Russell's *History of Western Philosophy,* really chewing over the ideas, is my ideal speed now."

Hirschberg confessed candidly in *The Priceless Gift* that discoursing with the immortals through their books was a compensation for an everyday life that was unsatisfactory in many ways.

I am stuck in the city, that's all I have. I am stuck in business and routine and tedium. But I give up only as much as I must; for the rest I live my life at its best, with art, music, poetry, literature, science, philosophy, and thought. I shall know the keener people of this world, think the keener thoughts, and taste the keener pleasures, as long as I can and as much as I can.

So this is the real practical use of self-education and self-culture. It converts a world which is only a good world for those who can win at its ruthless game into a world good for all of us. For your education is the only thing that nothing can take from you in this life. You can lose your money, your wife, your children, your friends, your pride, your honor, and your life, but while you live you can't lose your culture, such as it is.

Ted Marchi Learns How to Mend Roads

Quite another form of free learning is exemplified by Ted Marchi, a friend of many years who is now superintendent of public works for a medium-sized town in northern Nebraska. Now in his early sixties but looking a fast fifty (his name has been changed here or he'd be forced to retire), Marchi has spent his working lifetime "learning his living" by mastering worldly skills and trades quite the opposite from Hirschberg's preoccupations.

"The books on repair, maintenance, construction only take you so far," he observes, "never really get to *this* problem, *your* problem facing you right now. You're always left to figure out the 'why' in any particular case. *Why* won't this machine run? Where did this process break down? You get a feel for that by watching other men do it, feel it through your hands, absorb it by hanging around someone who can do it."

For Marchi, a high school dropout, his technical self-education started with an apprenticeship in boilermaking in 1929 at twenty-nine cents an hour. Later, when slot machines came into the county, Marchi found he could "hear" what was wrong with them and fix them by taking the machine apart and playing around with the parts. There were no books on this, of course, and in addition to the technical matters, Marchi was learning in whose favor the machines were "fixed."

In the late 1930s Marchi started working at a garage changing tires. He then learned how to change spark plugs and later mastered more advanced mechanics of auto repair. Marchi describes his learning process as "just watching, participating, talking shop. It seeped into my head and hands," he says, "and when I needed it, there it was. Don't get me wrong—I made plenty of mistakes. But those were wrong decisions of mine, and I learned from them more than if they'd been overexplained beforehand."

Moving up from garage work, Marchi went to work for the village, which, with many vehicles needing constant repair, had found it economical to employ a full-time mechanic. Once into the job, Marchi found that the village needed help in building roads too. He learned how to build them through his garage-tested method of watching, practice, mistakes, and perseverance.

Marchi is no engineer. The roads aren't perfect. But thanks to him the village has roads. It would have better roads had it waited for a highly trained engineer, but it now has adequate roads by using Ted, who *was* available. "My road-building methods are pretty primitive," he freely acknowledges. "They're based on feelings and common sense. If a problem seems unsolvable, I just quit for a day or so. Then, when my mind is rested, a solution always comes to me. What seemed so difficult yesterday seems simple today."

Marchi has now begun a new kind of learning: how to

play politics. "It's on-the-job training every day," he notes. "The technical part's the least of it. The more important part is what I call the battle of behavior—between what you have to say and do to get the official go-ahead for the job, and what's *really* needed. I've got to get along with the village board, a bunch of politicians who each wants more than his share of the credit for anything I do. But I can get out of them what I need to do my job, if I play my cards right. I'm still learning how to work that 'machine' for all it's worth!"

Like Cornelius Hirschberg, Ted Marchi is not an isolated case but an American type lost sight of in our confusion over diplomas versus learning. Men and women of Hirschberg's culture and Marchi's skill exist in virtually every part of the country. Only the modesty of their circumstances and, often, of their characters, makes them obscure. They revel in the use of the mind but haven't harnessed it for great profit or renown.

Tillie Lewis Learns to Grow Pomodoro Tomatoes—and Creates an Industry

In the 1930s Tillie Lewis saw her first can of pomodoros— pear-shaped tomatoes then grown only in Italy and imported into this country. Her husband carried the product in his Brooklyn wholesale grocery business. Using them in her own cooking for their extra tang, Mrs. Lewis began to wonder whether they could be grown in America. For one thing, she realized that the pomodoro was the critical ingredient in all the tomato pastes and tomato sauces imported in such quantities from Italy. If they could be grown in this country, they could be the key to a profitable new industry.

Her husband said no, the climate wasn't right. But Mrs. Lewis, intrigued by the idea, went to the Brooklyn Botanic Garden and sought out the experts. They too told her that both America's soil and climate were so different from Italy's that growing pomodoros in this country was impossible.

Undaunted, Mrs. Lewis wrote to the universities in Naples and Rome to get studies of soil, wind, and rain. She recalls, "I practically lived in the library for a while, reading everything that existed on the subject." In fact, her single-minded absorption contributed to the breakup of her marriage. Mrs. Lewis put herself through night school to study business methods, then she got a job selling securities. But the dream persisted. She saved her money and in 1934 booked passage to Italy.

On shipboard she met Florindo Del Gaizo, part owner of a Naples cannery that exported pomodoros. Gaizo was worried about a new U.S. tariff that he feared might put him out of business in this country. When Mrs. Lewis described her belief that pomodoros could be grown here, he invited her to his cannery and farms. The visit convinced her that sections of California had the soil and climate of southern Italy, where pomodoros could be grown. Gaizo agreed to stake her to seed, some old canning equipment, and $10,000.

The rest is food-industry history. The experiment succeeded, and Tillie Lewis Foods grew over the years into a $100 million–plus enterprise. When it was acquired in 1966 by the giant Ogden Corporation, she realized close to $9 million profit.

Mrs. Lewis made *Fortune*'s list of the ten highest-ranking businesswomen in 1973, received an honorary Doctor of Business Administration degree from the University of the Pacific, and was selected by *Ladies' Home Journal* as one of its Women of the Year in 1975.

Tillie Lewis's story is a paradigm of the American Dream in which winners made it up the ladder of success without boosts from prestigious schools. After examining the careers of outstanding people in business, the arts, politics, and other fields, social historian Caroline Bird recently concluded that "people who make it big in money, power, prestige, or achievement have always educated themselves in what they need to know. And they are still doing it today, whether they go to college or *not*." She notes that half of those described in *The Young Millionaires,* a 1973 book, never graduated from college.

Free learning does not just create "marketable skills" or a road to riches. Its rewards are more varied and important than that. In Mrs. Lewis's case, the intellectual curiosity and determination that fueled her business career still inform her life. Her current concern: the worldwide problem of hunger and nutrition.

"At my time of life I can afford to be reflective," she says at sixty-five. "And I'm worried; people don't understand the world food problem. How much more food do you think we can provide off the surface of this globe. While we sit talking, thousands of people are starving to death throughout the world.

"The problem of food is inextricably tangled with the problem of population. World population is increasing by 200,000 every day, which means that there are 75 million new mouths to feed annually. The only way this problem can be tackled is through a cooperative effort on the part of all nations. Nowadays, a shortage of one agricultural commodity in one part of the world has repercussions on how much of other commodities are available in other areas."

Tillie Lewis was the only female adviser on the American delegation to the historic conference held in Rome in 1968, sponsored by the United Nations Food and Agricultural Organization, to discuss ways to raise food standards throughout the world. She strongly advocates responsible action among her industry peers, insisting to groups like the Canners League of California that "We cannot view the American food industry without recognizing world food problems." The once-ardent learner has become an eloquent teacher of her peers.

Michael Rossman Learns to Make His Own Music

The goal of formal education has always been to produce people who could continue to learn on their own. But only recently have large numbers of college graduates taken up this challenge as a basic life-style. The so-called counter-culture of the late 1960s, which produced "free universities" on many campuses as alternatives to conventional college teaching, also created a vanguard of young adults who may presage the lifelong learner of the future.

Michael Rossman, who played a prominent part in the Free Speech movement at Berkeley, exemplifies these in-dividuals. Still writing and organizing in the San Francisco area, Rossman has described his experiences as a free learner in the booklet *Learning Without a Teacher* (Phi Delta Kappa, 1974), which he describes as "a record of a 'natural' process of learning, in which the learner was free to choose what and how he would learn." Not only does it portray a new kind of adult learner in action, it also shows how such learning flows readily and naturally from one realm of knowl-edge to another, in this case from music to politics.

A bad experience with being "taught" music in school turned Rossman off music entirely—until he heard Bach's flute sonatas during his first year at college.

The summer after an adolescent and turbid freshman year at the University of Chicago, I found an old recorder and locked myself in the bathroom for two months, learning to play from a simple instruction book. The pipe was badly out of tune, which didn't bother me—by then I couldn't even tell—but it drove my family wild, which was maybe part of the whole transaction. When I got back to school, I continued to practice regularly—not out of diligence, but in response to mood, a cer-tain tenor of lonesomeness that was good for at least half an hour of melody each twilight and often much longer, more ful-filling than solitaire if not much less aimless.

My models were the folksinger in the cafe, the string quartet. No one had ever suggested to me that playing to scratch an inner itch was musically legitimate, and for years I felt em-barrassed around "real" musicians. . . . I envied their technique, yet could not bear to practice scales and exercises, the traditional penance of the serious acolyte. At the time they bored me stiff; it took twelve years to get hip to some of their subtler joys.

Instead, as soon as I could read the high register and had some idea of tone, I tackled the real literature of the instrument. Its baroque emphasis offered an easy ladder of mastery, up through the heights of Telemann. I met the recorder's technical problems as they were integrated into music, and became proficient as rapidly as I might have through the grim student exercises that I continued to feel guilty about doing.

After his initial progress, Rossman reached out for other musicians to work with, a familiar pattern with independent learners.

Much of my learning came through playing with other musicians. When I left the bathroom I did the most useful thing possible: I organized a support group. The process now seems elegant; at the time it just sort of happened. I came back to school a fair player of folk tunes, starting on the classics, using the flauto dolce for self-definition and contact. Though inside I was all confused about my motivations, from outside I must have seemed simply unabashed enough to practice in public, for other players, some quite good, came out of hiding with their books of duets and asked to play together. Three months later a dozen of us were in casual afternoon association, just beginning on the quartet literature. I reread the student handbook: we were many enough to qualify as an official student group, and with a friend I organized the Recorder Society of the University of Chicago. Big deal? In a way, yes. Here an educational institution was functioning at its neutral best: it gave us a chance to meet each other, and then gave us precious open space to work together in—an old luxurious room, ours for two evenings a week. It also gave us its library, though whether its music teachers would have accepted us on our own terms is unlikely....

Together we learned the simple cooperations of group effort; shared our explorations of the literature; picked up trills, alternative fingerings and niceties of phrasing from the more advanced or more record-literate. So we all were wrapped in a community of learning, unselfconscious, open and supportive, whose fruit was not only good fellowship but the rapid development of consort skills, the power of collective work.

Later Rossman realized the significance of this first intensive experience with voluntary group learning. It had both educational and political implications:

It's always been hard to recognize and take seriously what nourishes me, and how I truly grew. My consort work was, quite simply, my first experience with sustained and disciplined investigation, by a voluntary and democratic group, of a subject that mattered to us. I spent twenty years in formal schooling—much of it even "enriched"—without being exposed to such experience.... So deep the hold of formal learning on our imagination, that it's taken me till thirty-and-three to recognize how important that experience was, independent of its particular subject, "music." Seven years free of the academy, a working intellectual, I see that it was a model for the two long cooperative investigations I've shared in since, and that it trained me for my part in them better than the schools ever did.

Helen Baker Learns to Be a Schoolyard Lawyer

Helen Baker of Shaker Heights, a Cleveland suburb, became a "schoolyard lawyer"—an effective advocate of the civil liberties of young people—by reading her way to a knowledge of the law and by fiercely following her impulse to right wrongs. When I met her some years ago Helen, now fifty-four, had involved herself as a volunteer with the Cleveland Civil Liberties Union's efforts on behalf of young people's rights. She participated in meetings and conferences, talked with experts, investigated actual conditions in schools, interviewed students. This work culminated in an article on the violations of civil liberties in American schools, published in the national newsletter of the American Civil Liberties Union.

"After the article appeared," Helen recalls, "some of the ACLU lawyers started asking me, 'Where did you get your law degree?' When I answered that I didn't have one, they would usually ask, 'Where do you work?' It turned out that what they were getting at was that I must work at a juvenile facility or have *some* professional place in the field. But as a matter of fact, I'd finally tell them, I'm what the census would label as a housewife. 'But how did you learn everything you had to know to write that article?' they would finally demand to know. And that's an interesting question, with a simple and useful answer. When I want to know something, I go and find out. When I wanted to find out about the statutes involving juveniles, I went and got hold of the statutes. It nearly killed me just to carry the damn book home. Then I kicked off my shoes, turned on the hi-fi, and started poring over the pages. Naturally, I couldn't make head or tail of some parts. But I knew that if John could understand those works, Jane could. So, back to Rule One: When you want to know, go find out! I started picking the brains of lawyers, and after several months I understood those statutes as well as they did, thanks partly to their help and partly to my determination."

Helen learned her self-imposed lessons well enough to begin championing the rights of young people in the schools of Cleveland and its suburbs. Realizing that the best way to achieve her purpose was to pass on what she knew, she wrote a simple handbook for parents and students. Now they could act as advocates themselves.

This handbook too became a learning project. "Doing something like that is so different from doing a paper or thesis for school or college," she points out. "For that handbook I had to understand the lingo of educational aims and objectives that the educators speak; I had to bone up on all the new approaches to school teaching, discipline, administration, and such; and I had to know the law concerning the rights of parents and the rights of students. I was told by one principal that I'd apparently read more in those fields, and actually put it to use, than some school administrators who go back for a doctorate. But it really was no strain because it was exactly what I wanted and needed to know, because I could put it right to use, and because no one was standing over me with a schedule and a grading system. If I messed up—and I certainly did, often—I'd just backtrack and catch up. Nobody had said that I had to master this stuff to *this* level by *this* date to take a goddamn test or submit my paper. It was all up to me. I could do it *right*—with 'right' being defined by my purposes."

Helen believes that her experiences have demonstrated what, for her, are the best ways of learning. "I'm not a 'collector' of learning, like some people collect jade, or paintings, or stamps. I'm interested in learning as something that improves and enhances the human condition—and not just my own. I'm less interested in learning for *myself*—although I obviously do some of that, since I write poetry and make silver jewelry, two fairly personal (for me) efforts. The handbook I did was to demystify the law so us everyday folks can get our hands on it. In order to help spread knowledge and techniques and *power*—and to seize that power from the professional elites who stand with their shotguns loaded with IQ tests, required courses, prerequisites, grades, diplomas, certification, double-think double-talk, to scare us out of their territory. Good fences may make good neighbors, but the fences of academe lock too many people out of control of their own learning and, thus, control of their own heads."

Marvin Weisbord Learns to Help People Change

Marvin Weisbord, a consultant from Wynnewood, Pennsylvania, learned to help other people change by changing himself. Ten years ago he was managing a business-forms company when he read Douglas McGregor's *The Human Side of Enterprise*. McGregor argued that employees would be more productive if they were treated as people who wanted to do well, take responsibility, grow, and do their best (Theory Y) rather than if they were subjected to the demeaning authoritarianism of the conventional firm (Theory X).

So Weisbord put Theory Y to the test. One Monday morning he reorganized his staff into five work teams of five people each. Each team was to handle a customer's print order from start to finish. "Teach each other your specialized jobs," he told them. "Just take care of the customers. Satisfy them however you feel best."

Unused either to freedom or responsibility, the employees panicked at solving problems previously solved by, or bucked to, their supervisors. The teams were begging for their supervisors back, but Weisbord held a series of meetings to solve the accumulated problems.

Through such long, frustrating meetings people began to learn to do their jobs in new ways. Weisbord was just at the point of giving up when finally the work groups began to click. Problems were solved where and when they occurred.

"Suddenly, I really understood what helping people to manage themselves was all about," Weisbord says. "I became aware that it took time and patience, required real problems *solved*, involved trial and error, and generated tremendous anxiety. I also began to understand—although I had no words for it then—what good teachers do instinctively: Structure the chance to learn, offer feedback and support, provide some tools and ideas, and stay out of the way.

"With a shock I realized the way I ran my business was anti-learning. I had no tolerance for mistakes. I wanted everything done right the first time—including the solutions to problems nobody had faced before.

"At last I understood what those thousands of Theory Y companies—all way ahead of me in the grim race I was running in my head—had learned in their expensive management-development courses. The name of the game was Theory Y, and I was playing catch-up.

"Little by little I turned it all over to the work teams—who to hire, who to fire, when to promote, what to give raises for (they decided the main criterion should be multiple skills, something that never had occurred to me), what equipment to buy, and how to schedule lunches and coffee breaks. So I was not terribly surprised when turnover (except for the ex-supervisors, who left early on) went to near zero and our order-processing capability jumped 40 per cent. Years later, I learned that those supposedly thousands of Theory Y firms in the mid-1960s eventually shook down to a dozen or so—and mine was one of them!

"The truth is if you don't put your ass on the line you can't grow at all."

Norman Macbeth Learns How Darwinism Died

Norman Macbeth was a retired lawyer and semi-invalid living in Switzerland in 1959, the centenary of the publication of Darwin's *Origin of Species*. "In an idle moment I picked up a volume of essays commemorating the event and read them straight through," he recalls.

"This was the beginning of my biological studies. In the next three years I continued in a random way by reading four paperbacks on evolution: Sir Julian Huxley, *Evolution in Action* (Mentor, 1957); John Maynard Smith, *The Theory of Evolution* (Penguin, 1958); Garrett Hardin, *Nature and Man's Fate* (Mentor, 1961); and Loren Eiseley, *Darwin's Century* (Doubleday Anchor, 1961)."

As a result of this reading, Macbeth noticed some striking contradictions between what he had understood biologists to believe about evolution and what these leading experts actually said. Prompted by these four paperbacks, he was stimulated to make further inquiries. "The next phase in my education took place over dinner tables. If conversation lagged, I asked friends whether they knew that Darwinism was going to pieces, that there was no struggle for existence, and that the scholars no longer spoke about the survival of the fittest. The responses were illuminating. They showed blind and universal faith in the doctrines learned many years earlier in college survey courses, and full conviction that the Scopes trial in Tennessee had laid all doubts to rest in 1925. My friends would not believe me without documentation. The conversation became lively.

"This led to the long and continuing third phase, in which I read the professional literature as well as popularizations and labored to put a coherent case on paper. I had to begin by sorting out the premises, including evolution itself."

Macbeth's learning project on evolutionary theory resulted in a brief book, *Darwin Retried* (Delta, 1973). Essentially a probing analysis of the four paperbacks he started with, his book argues that "classical Darwinism is dead" and that biologists no longer affirm the mechanisms of evolution that most of us still suppose to be true: survival of the fittest, adaptation, natural selection, the struggle for existence. Among those who have commended Macbeth's book is Sir Karl Popper, Professor Emeritus at the University of London. Although he does not accept the author's position, Popper called it "most meritorious and a really important contribution to the debate . . . a truly valuable book." Professor Jacques Barzun called it "a marvelous little work—compact, precise, lucid, and finally demonstrative."

What makes this case arresting is that evolutionary theory is one of the most complex fields of scientific inquiry. Professor Ernst Mayr of Harvard describes the fields considered requisite to comprehend the subject:

Genetics, morphology, biogeography, systematics, paleontology, embryology, physiology, ecology, and other branches of biology, all have illuminated some special aspect of evolution and have contributed to the total explanation where other special fields failed. In many branches of biology one can become a leader even though one's knowledge is essentially confined to an exceedingly limited area. This is unthinkable in evolutionary biology. A specialist can make valuable contributions to special aspects of the evolutionary theory, but only he who is well versed in most of the above-listed branches of biology can present a balanced picture of evolution, as a whole.

Macbeth is not unique. Despite ever narrowing specialization, perceptive amateurs continue to produce worthwhile work in many fields. Charles M. Fair did it in philosophy with *The Dying Self*, Eric Hoffer in political science with *The True Believer*, George Dennison in education with *The Lives of Children.*

Such people are "avocational academics" (a term suggested by Loring Thompson of Northeastern University)— individuals with other than academic professions who pursue learning, and often achieve publishable results, just for the fun of it.

Modern economic affluence is now making scholarly endeavors possible as a way of life open to all who are interested [Thompson points out]. People now have the freedom to select important, major interests and devote much of their lives to these interests, regardless of employment opportunities. In fact to pursue a creative or artistic interest as a vocation may be more frustrating than to pursue it with the freedom of avocation, because employees must be responsible for conformance with market demands, corporate policies, and burdensome administrative details.

My point here is not that all of us can contribute to the body of human knowledge or write outstanding books, but rather that intellectual accomplishment is not the exclusive domain of traditional academic scholarship.

In other fields too the gifted amateurs have achieved dramatic results. Thor Heyerdahl believed that Africans and Egyptians crossed the Atlantic in papyrus boats, bringing the culture and technology of the Old World to South America centuries before Columbus. When the scientific establishment denied that such crossings were possible, Heyerdahl assembled craftsmen who could still build papyrus boats, verified their proper construction with ancient drawings and sculptures, and finally successfully faced the rigors of the sea.

Heyerdahl contributed to the picture of man's historical

development not through library and laboratory research but through a tenacious inquiry into the realities of papyrus, sea, tides, weather, and human stamina. No expert on papyrus boats he consulted had ever seen or sailed such a boat. Like Macbeth's, Heyerdahl's was a project in free learning. In both, independent minds confronted the academic establishment, and found their own way to real and important truths.

Some of the best opportunities for non-professional scholars and thinkers lie in addressing a large public on some issue that full-time academics consider beneath their notice. For example, many scientists felt for years that a refutation needed to be written of the jerry-built speculations of Erich von Däniken. His best sellers like *Chariots of the Gods?* had promulgated the theory that this earth had been visited in times past by astronauts from highly advanced extraterrestrial civilizations who had mated with earth creatures to produce an improved breed and then departed. The book clicked with the UFO and occult crowds, and sold 34 million copies throughout the world.

Serious scientists grumbled over their sherry but failed to generate a coherent response. "It took an amateur to come forth with a sustained book-length attack on von Däniken's theories and evidence," the New York *Times* reported in mid-1976 when the first such work appeared. Ronald Story, who works for the Tucson, Arizona, Gas and Electric Company, had taken up the cudgels and collated the previous attacks on von Däniken, adding some devastating new criticisms of his own.

When he wrote for help to some leading figures in the field, they were so excited at his enterprise that they offered enthusiastic support. Thor Heyerdahl had long been bothered by von Däniken's argument that the statues on Easter Island could not have been built without extraterrestrial help, and he contributed a long statement to the book on this point. Carl Sagan, a most renowned researcher into life on other planets, volunteered to write a foreword because he was delighted that someone was taking the time to give von Däniken his just desserts. "Which all goes to show," the *Times* observed, "that sometimes amateurs can barge in where experts are too aloof to tread."

As this book goes to press, Alex Haley's *Roots* has inspired a whole new area of amateur scholarship. Hundreds of thousands of Americans, inspired by Haley's tireless quest for his family's history, are delving into their own past, discovering that, in Charles Beard's forgotten phrase, every man can indeed be his own historian.

Barbara Andrus Learns How to Help Troubled Teenagers— and Earns a B.A.

Barbara Andrus, a thirty-eight-year-old mother of four, is a veteran community worker and organizer in the North Minneapolis community, the section of the city with the greatest minority population. She is currently director of a group home for troubled teenage women, a job she enjoys and finds socially useful.

About two years ago Mrs. Andrus began to feel the need for some additional skills to make her program work better for the people it served. "I was struggling with how to formulate some sensible evaluation plan for the program," she recalls. "The husband of a woman who works with me suggested one evening that I'd benefit greatly from some input from the University—and also that there was a program through which I could be earning a degree for the learning I was going to be doing."

Mrs. Andrus had never gotten a B.A. and didn't particularly feel the need for one in her work and life. But the advice stimulated her to look into the "University Without Walls" program at the University of Minnesota. This was a "contract learning" program, in which there was no predetermined curriculum, each student creating his own. In this case, the Minnesota program proved to have an important place in Barbara Andrus's project of learning how to do her job better.

"I discovered I'd only have to take classes that suited my goals and needs, and I'd be moving toward the degree through all kinds of learning I was doing in the rest of my life. At my age, and with a full-time job, it would have taken me five years to get a degree in a conventional program—and what good would it have done me anyway?"

Her aspirations were matched by the views of Jeff Johnson, director of the program. "We were looking for people like Barbara," he says. "We wanted individuals who had shown they were self-starters, were highly motivated, and had the guts to try something new and a little dangerous, where they wouldn't know ahead of time what were the exact requirements for the degree but were confident they could handle it."

"The first thing I learned about the program," Barbara says, "is that it started with *me*—not with some curriculum I had to fit into. Practically everything I've done in working towards the degree has been something I've wanted or needed to do either for my personal or professional development. Rather than feeling like time *out*, it's seemed like a way to get more deeply and creatively into my deepest concerns.

"Once I'd identified my learning goals," Mrs. Andrus continues, "we reviewed my life-experiences to identify things I'd already learned—learning I could demonstrate, and that had moved me towards my degree objectives. My former bosses, colleagues, and officials I've worked with in the community have done detailed evaluations of what I've learned and can do.

"After determining what I already knew, we worked out my actual program. This boiled down to a series of 'learning contracts,' each of which was to involve specified readings, research, writing, and sometimes other work. For example, in the course of one contract I completed the draft of a training manual I'm writing, distributed it to a number of experts and fellow practitioners for evaluation and suggestions, and also tested it out on a pilot group of students."

Naturally, the ways in which students are evaluated in contract learning programs must be quite different from conventional testing, grading, and credentialing. With each student's program being unique, the ways in which progress is measured and the criteria for graduation must also derive from each candidate's distinctive objectives. So each learning contract has an evaluation process built in, which may range from a detailed report from an employer or supervisor of what has been accomplished and learned in a work or internship experience, to a paper analyzing or applying a group of readings, or a product such as an artwork judged by a group of experts.

Final graduation is usually based on a major project embodying much of what has been learned. For Barbara Andrus, it will be the completion and validation—through field testing and expert evaluation—of her training manual for directors of the kind of facility she is successfully operating. "I think it will be a real improvement over what's been available before," she says. "This is the first time that training materials like this have been prepared by a person like myself, who is working at the job, living in the community, and who—being black and having been poor—knows the people's problems from my own experiences."

Free learners who want to pursue their studies even more independently than Barbara Andrus can find programs through which they can earn a degree without ever having to come to a campus. Nicholas France, who received his diploma in 1974 at the age of twenty-seven, was the first of thousands who have done this.

While serving in the army in 1965, France had taken the United States Armed Forces Institute college-equivalency exams, a five-hour battery of tests. His good marks earned him three semesters of college credit.

After the army, France started work in New York for the U.S. Treasury regional administrator of national banks. As a financial intern, he learned banking and accounting on the job. One day on a library bulletin board he saw a poster advertising the Regents External Degree Program.

For ten dollars he enrolled in the business administration program. He received a couple of forty-page mimeographed study guides, purchased twenty books or so, and studied on his own for about two years. When he was ready, in September 1974, France took the eleven-hour set of exams that New York State requires of candidates for the degree. He made it. Total cost for his college education: about $410.

"We figure he knows just about as much as the graduate of a traditional college," says Robert Anstett, registrar of the program. "That's what the exam's designed to test."

"I had a little trouble with the Treasury Department," France admits, "when I told them I'd soon have my degree through this method. They asked if it was a correspondence course, which they won't accept. But when I told them that the State of New York would certify the degree, they said it was O.K."

On the basis of his degree, France was promoted from financial intern to assistant national bank examiner and received a $2000 raise.

"I could never have managed to go back to a regular college," says France. "With a wife and child and a full-time job, I would have been behind the eightball for the rest of my life for lack of that diploma. This kind of program gives people like me a second chance for success." France is currently pursuing a master's degree at Iona College in New York in his spare time.

Nicholas France symbolizes a new option for free learners —the chance to cash in their learning for credits leading to a college degree. In our credential-crazy society many people understandably feel the need for this kind of recognition. So if you have the knowledge, understanding, and skill of college graduates who are routinely given preference for jobs, turn to page 158 for information on how to obtain credits and a degree through "Show What You Know" programs.

Malcolm X Learns "The Truth About the Black Man's Role"

Malcolm X acquired his "homemade education" while serving time in the Norfolk Prison Colony.

In every free moment I had [he reports in his *Autobiography*], if I was not reading in the library, I was reading in my bunk. You couldn't have gotten me out of books with a wedge. Between Mr. Muhammad's teachings, my correspondence, my visitors— usually Ella and Reginald—and my reading of books, months passed without my even thinking about being imprisoned. In fact, up to then I never had been so truly free in my life.

The curriculum of Malcolm's self-education grew directly out of his concerns and commitments.

Once I heard of the "glorious history of the black man," I took special pains to hunt in the library for books that would inform me on details about black history. . . .

I found books like Will Durant's *Story of Civilization*. I read H. G. Wells' *Outline of History. Souls of Black Folk* by W. E. B. Du Bois gave me a glimpse into the black people's history before they came to this country. Charles G. Woodson's *Negro History* opened my eyes about black empires before the black slave was brought to the United States, and the early Negro struggles for freedom.

J. A. Rogers' three volumes of *Sex and Rape* told about race-mixing before Christ's time; about Aesop being a black man who told fables; about Egypt's Pharaohs; about the great Coptic Christian Empires; about Ethiopia, the earth's oldest continuous black civilization, as China is the oldest continuous civilization.

When I discovered philosophy, I tried to touch all the landmarks of philosophical development. Gradually, I read most of the old philosophers. Occidental and Oriental. The Oriental philosophers were the ones I came to prefer; finally my impression was that most Occidental philosophy had largely been borrowed from the Oriental thinkers. Socrates, for instance, traveled in Egypt. Some sources even say that Socrates was initiated into some of the Egyptian mysteries. Obviously Socrates got some of his wisdom among the East's wise men.

Malcolm's reading didn't come without cost. He had arrived at Norfolk with 20/20 vision; by the time he left, the detrimental conditions under which he had studied had led to astigmatism and the need for the glasses he was to wear till his death. The account of the prison conditions which made study so harrowing cannot fail to remind us of Abraham Lincoln's fabled self-education by the glow of his family's flickering hearth:

When I had progressed to really serious reading, every night at about ten P.M. I would be outraged with the "lights out." It always seemed to catch me right in the middle of something engrossing.

Fortunately, right outside my door was a corridor light that cast a glow into my room. The glow was enough to read by, once my eyes adjusted to it. So when "lights out" came, I would sit on the floor where I could continue reading in that glow.

At one-hour intervals the night guards paced past every room. Each time I heard the approaching footsteps, I jumped into bed and feigned sleep. And as soon as the guard passed, I got back out of bed onto the floor area of that light-glow where I would read for another fifty-eight minutes—until the guard approached again. That went on until three or four every morning. Three or four hours of sleep a night was enough for me. Often in the years in the streets I had slept less than that.

I know of no more eloquent tribute to the potential of self-education than Malcolm's final reflection on the importance of reading in his life:

I have often reflected upon the new vistas that reading opened to me. I knew right there in prison that reading had changed forever the course of my life. As I see it today, the ability to read awoke inside me some long dormant craving to be mentally alive. I certainly wasn't seeking any degree the way a college confers a status symbol upon its students. My homemade education gave me, with every additional book that I read, a little bit more sensitivity to the deafness, dumbness, and blindness that was afflicting the black race in America. Not long ago, an English writer telephoned me from London, asking questions. One was, "What's your alma mater?" I told him, "Books." You will never catch me with a free fifteen minutes in which I'm not studying something I feel might be able to help the black man.

Malcolm reminds me of the free learner who led this gallery, Cornelius Hirschberg. He too took all of culture as his province. He too relied on books because they were his only available conduit to the best that has been thought and felt.

But there is a crucial difference. Whereas Hirschberg found in the verbal world of beauty and truth a compensation for his drab daily life, Malcolm seized on history and philosophy as tools of liberation. For him, self-education strengthened the striving for justice, for himself and his people.

Chapter 3 / ''A WAY TO BE'': LEARNING IN OUR LIVES

Learning is not a task or a problem—it is a way to be in the world. Man learns as he pursues goals and projects that have meaning for him.

—SIDNEY JOURARD

Learning as "a way to be" is a new notion to most people. We readily see ourselves in other distinct roles: son or daughter, breadwinner, parent, even citizen. In these roles we seem to have a sense of our own development, of the growth of these various "selves" over the years. But our growth as learners often eludes us. We know we change, but we are not aware that the *ways* in which we change themselves change. At different stages of life we use different means of monitoring the outside world, mastering new skills, and reshaping our personalities.

Heightened awareness of learning as a "way to be" strengthens us in moving toward what we wish to become.

The Prevalence of Lifelong Learning

In the last decade, social scientists have begun to examine the extent to which adults pursue learning on their own. The findings are heartening:

- Most people, it turns out, do engage in purposeful "learning projects" quite regularly, and go about them in an interesting diversity of ways.

- The adult's approach to learning is quite different from that of the child.
- Adults' successive acts of learning fit into patterns of growth and development that are almost as clear as the familiar stages of childhood, though more diversified.

The first national survey of adults' educational pursuits, *Volunteers for Learning*, published in 1965, revealed that millions of adults in the United States—one person in every five—had engaged in at least one self-instruction project during the preceding year. When asked if they had ever tried to teach themselves something since leaving school, almost twice as many answered yes. Moreover, in some fields this was by far the preferred mode of learning. For example, 80 percent of all those learning home improvement, gardening, hobbies, and other technical skills taught themselves. "The category [of self-teaching] may well represent the most overlooked avenue of activity in the whole field of adult education," the survey concluded, noting that its extent was "surprising" and "much greater than anticipated."

More recent evidence appeared in 1972, when a Carnegie Corporation–sponsored study found that three out of four American adults wanted to "learn more about something" or to "do something better." Most of them said they wanted to study something that would advance them in their work, but the second largest group wanted to master some hobby or recreational skill.

So it is not surprising to find out that thirty million adults —one person out of every five—are currently enrolled in some form of education or training. The "Joe College" eighteen- to twenty-two-year-old is no longer the norm; one-third of all students attending college are now adults returning to the campus. They have created a back-to-school boom that has saved many a college from bankruptcy as the "college-age" enrollment has dwindled over the past several years.

From these survey results it seems fair to conclude that the closer you look at adult learning, the more learning you find. Canadian researcher Allen Tough has pioneered in systematically scrutinizing adults' independent learning. Tough's studies and others have confirmed the extraordinary extent of this kind of learning. Nearly *every* adult, it now appears, undertakes some such project each year. These researches also provide revealing clues as to the nature of free learning.

Most self-education, Tough has discovered, is not undertaken with an eye to academic credit, and for this reason most of the people surveyed at first hesitated to believe that what they'd been doing could be called learning. Adults are apt to dismiss from the "education" category independent ventures that have taught them as much as or more than they could have learned in a classroom. Such is the myopia induced by our national fixation on credits and credentials.

My own observations underscore this point. The reluctance of the self-taught to honor their own enterprise mirrors the attitude that—until very recently—has prevailed in the universities, corporations, and professions. "Degrees are used as fly swatters," one of the self-taught told me, "to kill unpapered people." Fortunately, in the 1970s this attitude has been changing as pragmatic self-interest, if nothing more humane, persuades the Establishment to honor actual capacity and performance.

Tough discovered something more than that free learning is commonplace. He found a small group of exceptionally active "high" learners:

The members of this group are especially competent, efficient, and successful at learning. They probably set clear action goals, choose appropriate knowledge and skill, plan for their learning episodes fairly easily, and learn without undue effort or frustration. They are marked by efforts to achieve their inherent potential, and by curiosity and *joie de vivre*. Yet, at the same time, these people like their present job, understand and accept their own characteristics, and are not strongly dissatisfied with their present self. They have the confidence and courage to reveal their real self. They have clearly directed interests: they choose their own career and activities and are not pushed by external forces. They have a strong but realistic commitment to some mission in life. They strive to achieve certain major goals, are spurred on rather than blocked by obstacles, and are productive and successful. Their relationship with at least a few people tends to be compassionate, loving, frank, and effective.

Tough's "high" learners are strikingly like the ideal "self-actualized" individual that today's humanistic psychologists have described. John Gardner summed it up best when he evoked the image of the individual capable of self-renewal, for whom "the development of his own potentialities and the process of self-discovery never end. Exploration of the full range of his own potentialities is not something that self-renewing man leaves to the chances of life. It is something he pursues systematically, or at least avidly, to the end of his days. He looks forward to an endless and unpredictable dialogue between his potentialities and the claims of life—not only the claims he encounters but the claims he invents."

Significantly the empirical research of the social scientists and the theoretical speculations of the psychologists converge here, at the top: The supremely healthy individual is a lifelong learner.

The Varieties of Lifelong Learning

Most of us who have been "educated" tend to be biased, consciously or not, toward learning that is bookish and verbal. I am no exception. Until I began the self-education that resulted in this book, the free learners I celebrated were, typically, bookish. I, who derided snobbery and short-sightedness in the educational establishment, had blandly ignored the process whereby countless people gain mastery of the skills that fascinate most Americans—things like carpentry, auto mechanics, plumbing, sewing, gardening, cooking, sailing, sports of all kinds.

But my research over the past five years has forced me to

broaden my outlook. Interviewing free learners throughout the country, I've found Americans learning virtually every kind of subject, from job-related skills to science and music. The subjects have included radio announcing, philosophy, freelance writing, educational administration, secretarial work, conducting social science surveys, civil liberties law, landscape painting, financial planning, cartooning, electrical repairs, farming, astronomy, anatomy, mathematics, linguistics, basic English, the cello.

D. L. Pertz of Pine Brook, New Jersey, and her husband taught themselves how to build their three-bedroom ranch house. Ray Walker of Nashville mastered courtroom stenography, out of which he has created a thriving business. Joy Figueiredo of San Francisco probed telepathic communication by dissecting animals' brains in her home laboratory. Phyllis Herde of Lawndale, California, learned how to run a small business. Chester Johns of Livonia, Michigan, learned to speak effectively through a local speaking club and now does it professionally. Jerry Maltz of Encino, California, explored philosophy on his own, since "only you can ask yourself the deeper questions of life." David Feign of Santa Ana, California, became an aerodynamics engineer, then pioneered in the computer field—a field in which he *had* to teach himself, because at that point there weren't any teachers of the subject.

The list could continue indefinitely, filling much of this book. Let me just mention a couple more of my favorites. Suse Field of Richmond, Virginia, and her husband have taught themselves how to recognize and collect rare books. "Neither one of us knew much about rare books when we first got married," she recalls. "Now we know quite a bit and enjoy it thoroughly. At present I am working on the process of marbeling, or marbelizing, papers, which is a method used to apply color and patterns to paper by floating color on a solution and picking it up by dipping paper. Many old books were bound in such papers. I am interested in modernizing the design and the process and simply seeing how far one can go with it." The Fields' learning suggests that do-it-yourself education need not be lonely.

"Many people have acquired proficiency in a field of endeavor simply by association with it as, for example, apprentices," notes Brinto Carson of York, Pennsylvania. "Despite the fact that I did not complete a second year at the University of Pennsylvania, having flunked all my science courses, I am now a civil engineer, a life member of the American Society of Civil Engineers and many other major professional associations, and was for ten years an associate professor at Drexel Institute as well as head of the Civil Engineering Section, Naval Reserve Officers School."

Consistently, my research has revealed the personal character of free learning, with each person doing what he is uniquely equipped to do—determining precisely what he wants, when and how and where he wants it. Another common thread, confirmed as well by Tough's and other broad-based surveys, is the primacy of other *people* as learning resources. Though occasionally they may be paid experts, they are more often friends, neighbors, relatives, or colleagues. Chances are most of us prefer to learn *with* other people, if not necessarily *from* them. (Later I will provide specifics on the many communal ways to set up or join learning projects—from the mentor, in a one-to-one situation, to learning exchanges and social action initiatives, to the more formal offerings and services of free universities, educational brokers, and the non-traditional study programs increasingly available from formal institutions.)

The Rhythm of Learning

All learning has a basic pattern, whether a week's encounter with an intriguing new book or a year's work in anthropology, surveying, or needlepoint. Alfred North Whitehead identified it as "the rhythm of education" in his essay of that title in *The Aims of Education.*

Whitehead pointed out that it is a mistake to assume

that progress in mastering any new subject or skill is "a uniform steady advance." Rather, the drama of learning tends to be played out in three acts: romance, precision, and generalization.

In the first stage, romance, "the subject matter has the vividness of novelty," Whitehead explains. One merely has "glimpses" that are "half-concealed by the wealth of material." "In this stage learning is not dominated by systematic procedures," he observes. Instead it is sparked by romantic emotion. Whitehead illustrates the point from *Robinson Crusoe:* "Crusoe was a mere man, the sand was mere sand, the footprint was a mere footprint and the island was a mere island, and Europe was the busy world of men. But the sudden perception of the half-disclosed and half-hidden possibilities relating Crusoe and the sand and the footprint and the lonely island secluded from Europe constitutes romance."

Whitehead's stage of romance is a familiar one to most people with active minds. We feel it when plunging into a new challenge or problem, discovering a new author who illuminates our life, or visiting a foreign country.

In the second stage of the learning process, which Whitehead called "precision," inchoate visions and impulses take on more exact form. We seek techniques to learn more; we analyze facts bit by bit. "The facts of romance have disclosed ideas with possibilities of wide significance, and ... we acquire other facts in a systematic order," Whitehead explains.

The third stage in Whitehead's cycle is generalization, "a return to romanticism with added advantage of classified ideas and relevant technique." Here the informed mind, well-stocked with experiences—direct and vicarious— achieves the end of all learning: creative thought and action. For while the first two stages of learning emphasize receptivity, openness, and the capacity to absorb knowledge, the culmination should be synthesis, application, and action. The free learner is not merely entranced by new realms of knowledge, nor interested simply in developing his capacity to appreciate and understand them. He or she finds the ultimate reward in the excitement of exercising the power that real learning engenders.

Lest our learning begin to seem too predictable according to this underlying rhythm, let's frankly acknowledge the element of luck. It plays a major role in adult learning, because the non-institutionalized learner is not constrained to a fixed curriculum. He can follow his nose, chasing shamelessly after appealing scents. Sometimes these will be dead ends, but amazingly often they will prove even more rewarding than the path on which one was set at the start.

A friend's chance remark may introduce an absorbing new writer, or a newspaper item may lead to a useful or intriguing interest. Those free learners par excellence—artists, writers, musicians, and other exceptionally creative people —know that some of their happiest ideas come as gifts.

Author-longshoreman Eric Hoffer describes how he does "research": "I go to the library, I pick up the things that interest me, I use whatever comes my way. . . . I depend on chance to help me find what I need, and most of the time I've been lucky." No wonder that creative artists have kept their faith in the muse, that fickle divinity who sometimes bestows inspiration and sometimes withholds it, and whose favor cannot be commanded.

This serendipitous element in learning is exemplified in William Glasser's account of how he discovered "positive addiction" (PA), his term for any habit—like running or playing the piano or transcendental meditation—that has the opposite effect of negative addictions such as drink or smoking or drugs. Positive addictions add to the individual's strength and energy rather than debilitating him. Glasser advocates that everyone should try to develop such an addiction.

The discovery of PA began serendipitously. In the summer of 1973, while on vacation, Glasser read in Roger Kahn's delightful book *The Boys of Summer* an anecdote about

George "Shotgun" Shuba, who explained that his "natural swing" was developed by swinging a weighted bat six hundred times every day of his life.

When I read that anecdote and visualized Shuba swinging that bat six hundred times [reports Glasser], something went ping in my mind.... I said to myself, how did he do it? How did he keep it up?... What then ran through my mind ... was the only way he could have done it was far beyond what we usually call will-power. If all he had was will-power I don't believe he could have gone on so long; there had to be something else; and right then, although I hadn't any idea how, I came to the conclusion that what had happened was that he became addicted to swinging the bat. The idea of being hooked on bat swinging seemed silly and when I shared the idea with my family we all laughed but I still couldn't get it out of my head. It doesn't seem silly now, because after thinking about this idea almost obsessively for the next eighteen months, I believe that is exactly what happened.

Glasser did more than brood about the idea. He went out and gathered information and further insights about it. "I began to ask for reactions about positive addiction from the audiences to whom I frequently speak. [Dr. Glasser lectures widely on his system of Reality Therapy.] After a regular talk I would give a short description of PA and then ask people who thought they were positively addicted to meet with me afterward and tell me about their experiences." This led him to a wealth of further evidence, perceptions, and understanding about the phenomenon.

Luck struck continually, spurring further research. An article in *Psychology Today* prompted him to write to the authors for additional data. Having noted that runners compose a large proportion of the positively addicted, he put a notice in the magazine *Running World* asking readers to fill out a rather extensive form. Glasser expected a limited response. "I was not prepared for the avalanche that descended upon me—almost seven hundred replies from a subscription list of twenty thousand." His survey asked,

"Do you suffer if you miss a run? Do you always enjoy your run?" The answer from the addicts was mostly a strong yes. Glasser's conclusion, briefly, was that if you become addicted to certain activities to the point that they become pleasurable, compulsive habits, you can derive exhilaration, energy, and strength from them that you can transfer to other tasks.

The result of this research was the book *Positive Addiction* (Harper & Row, 1976). What is interesting here is the simplicity of Glasser's methods, which are available, in principle, to any free learner: extrapolating from one's reading, talking, and reflecting about promising ideas; gathering data from people; following up on related leads (the *Psychology Today* article); soliciting additional data. Glasser's is an intriguing new concept in practical psychology, developed not through specialized laboratory techniques but by energetically pursuing an original insight—and a little bit of luck.

Of course, such luck comes most readily when we have prepared for it. The free learner who has sharpened his awareness, heightened his alertness to certain subjects, and has begun putting himself in the way of fresh materials, situations, experiences, and people will inevitably begin to have more and more "accidental" learnings. As friends and colleagues become aware of our interest in certain fields, they begin calling things to our attention. As we make connections between our subject and others, more and more items become relevant.

Whoever is the muse of free learners, she favors those who have paid her homage. The more you plan to learn, the more unplanned learning will come your way as a gift.

Adults as Learners

Adults as learners are quite different from young people, which is why educators come a cropper when they try to use child-oriented teaching techniques on grownups. Adults have a fuller, richer, more stable and autonomous sense of self than children do, and a repertoire of experiences from which to draw as they read, discuss, create, and experiment. (Plato thought that young people could not understand or practice politics because they lacked sufficient experience in human affairs.)

An adult's motivation to learn is different from a child's. Adults are less willing than children to accept on the authority of a teacher that what they are learning will prove its worth later in life. Adults' sense of urgency is different; they want faster results because of all the conflicting demands on their time. And they usually have an idea of what they need to learn.

For example, people in their early thirties are characteristically fixated on "making it" in the world of work. What they learn tends to center around the skills they need in order to advance occupationally. Later most people go through a kind of "second adolescence" around the age of forty. They become absorbed with other potentialities: reviving their capacity for intimacy and emotional growth. In the later years, as the demands of raising a family and achieving financial security abate for the successful, adults frequently find that exploring the arts and humanities grows more compelling. And interwoven with these broad general human patterns of changing interest is the ad hoc channeling brought about by specific changes in one's own life: a move to a new location, the decision to change occupations, an overwhelming interest in a subject or a cause. Any of these can spark and sustain new directions in an individual's learning.

Adulthood is not a plateau on which the personality formed by earlier experiences is merely played out against changing circumstances. Rather, the adult years have their own drama of development, their new crises of growth and change, which are just as decisive as those of childhood and youth. The one thing that does not change is the fact of change.

What is most heartening about recent findings—documented in Erik Erikson's seminal writings and brought up to date in Gail Sheehy's book *Passages*—is the thesis that these crises of adult life, squarely met and surmounted, foster growth and development that can lead to new heights of understanding and accomplishment.

But what about the process of aging? Here, above all, myths abound—of atrophy, decline, collapse. Many people from middle age on are dogged by the unwarranted fear of mental decline. They've been brainwashed especially by notions about the memory failure that age allegedly brings, or the progressive inability to learn new things. Though psychological studies—to say nothing of ordinary observation—have quite exploded these myths, they are still widely enough accepted to act often as self-fulfilling prophecies. If people believe they can't learn, they very well may not.

But continuing to use one's mind and senses keeps them sharp and makes them sharper. *The Ulyssean Adult* is the provocative title of the best book on this subject. John A. B. McLeish, the author, believing that we can be creative until our dying days, provides hundreds of examples of men and women in all kinds of circumstances who have done just that.

Learning, then, is indeed a much larger part of our lives than has been thought. In fact, it seems fair to go further and suggest that learning—purposeful self-change—is the cutting edge of our personal development. It is the way we invest time and energy in our own growth. It is our way of making and remaking ourselves, in small ways and large, throughout our lives.

While the effects of heredity, environment, and early conditioning cannot be denied, this continuing capacity to change and grow is equally important. Moreover, such changes do not require special treatment or intervention. We tend to assume that the only way an adult can really learn to act in new ways, acquire important new capacities, or grow substantially in any direction is by taking time out for a formal educational program or intensive therapy or by making a radical change in his occupation or dwelling place.

But there are other powerful ways to alter and reshape oneself. While dramatic intervention may be called for from time to time, far more important is day-to-day, week-to-week expansion of awareness, interests, and learning capability.

In learning how to manage this process efficiently and enjoyably, we are learning the secret of transforming ourselves gradually into the people we would like to be.

"What is a good learner?" asks Michael Rossman in *On Learning and Social Change*. "It seems useful to think of him with a certain set of skills. He knows how to formulate problems. He can identify the relevant resources, of information or whatever, that are available in his environment. He is able to choose or create procedures and to evaluate his results."

These skills and the ways to acquire them quickly and easily are what the rest of the book is about. Not only can we learn all manner of things worth knowing and doing and becoming, we can also learn how to learn better.

Chapter 4 / LEARNING, HOW TO

> *The way of the masters was to find their own way.*
>
> —ZEN PROVERB

Enough theory. The rest of this book—except for a final chapter on certain social implications of self-education—tells how you can begin or, if you've already started, how you can enhance the process of your own free learning. "I know, at fifty-seven, that *I learn faster and easier than ever before*," Cornelius Hirschberg wrote in his autobiography. "There are techniques to this learning business, and I am getting better at it. Today I open up a new subject, and the whole strength of everything I have learned up to now moves in to help me. Mathematicians will understand what I mean when I say that everything you learn acts as a constant and even an increasing accelerating force *provided you set it free to move.* Therefore, your *velocity* of learning steadily increases as you keep on doing it."

You as a Learner

The first technique is to apply, in particular and fairly simple ways, the difficult advice mankind has been getting from seers and sages down the centuries: Know thyself. All I'm suggesting is that you begin to pay attention to yourself as a changing, developing, and growing person. Notice how you behave in different situations, how you respond to different people and problems.

Focusing so much on yourself may sound self-indulgent. Yet it is only by listening to such stirrings (which we are usually in too much of a hurry to hear) that we can identify what concerns us most.

Learning, How to

Design your own education. Though your goals may change over time, you must begin somewhere. Start with exploring how you learn best and what's most worth learning for you right now. You're the boss as a free learner; you can take command of your own education: what, where, when, how, and with whom you will learn.

Start a learning log. Everyone is learning all the time, for good or bad. Although many experiences can nourish your ability to grow, you lose their full value if you don't pay enough attention to what's happening. Your learning log will help ensure that nothing valuable is wasted and that your learning becomes cumulative, enabling you to take full advantage of every kind of experience.

Take advantage of the Invisible University. Being taught in a classroom is just one way to learn. Society brims with more convenient and more economical ways. Millions of people today are discovering the joys of independent learning; most of them prefer to learn together. There are ways you can find and join up with co-learners in your community.

To tune in to yourself most effectively, imagine how you might change—develop new skills, interests, capacities—

over the next month or year. Look backward too. Consider yourself as you are today and as you were a year ago, five years ago. Recall some things and ways you've learned, either in or out of school, that you found either particularly pleasant or particularly awful. Your answers should clue you in to how you learn best. In isolation or in company? From books, other media, teachers, fellow students? Are you one who plunges into the sea and just begins to swim, lest otherwise you drown? Or would you rather watch the proficient swimmers and try the water by slow degrees? Who knows? Only you.

A novel device comes from Ari Kiev, a psychiatrist, who suggests to patients that for a month they clip all the newspaper articles that catch their interest, and then inspect the collection to see if a pattern of interest emerges. Dr. Kiev also urges them to keep alert to the slightest indications of special skills or talents, even those that seem silly. Such devices help his patients to get back in touch with affinities they have suppressed. (You may, of course, have the opposite problem—all too many interests, so that you're dissipating your energies with dilettantism. If so, the learning log will enable you to begin sorting, consolidating, and giving focus to your divergent interests.)

Having defined your interests and enthusiasms, use them. "The road to new interests is the natural route of fascination and delight," writer Hilton Gregory says, noting that people who keep finding such interests "don't make reaching out a chore ... they do not drearily *drive* themselves to self-improvement. True, any line of inquiry diligently pursued is preferable to ennui; but what we need are sustaining, rather than sustained, interests. A leisurely approach that trusts spontaneous curiosity permits our faculties to soar."

Gregory suggests definite strategies for cultivating such enthusiasms. "We have all enjoyed moments of unaccountable good feeling," he observes, when "work does itself; we feel strong and confident; problems shrink." We must learn to take the current when it serves. "There are around us every day thermals of interest," he notes, referring to the "thermals" sailplanes use to cruise the air. "A penetrating book or conversation with a new friend can propel us to maneuvering heights." Cultivating your interests and riding them isn't self-indulgence. It's healthy to act on impulses to expand your knowledge and understanding. Such growth in a person's interests and activities is natural. But as with all natural growth, we must make the time for it—not force it, but gently cultivate it.

A cautionary tale. You will not be able to excel at everything you would like to learn. One friend of mine knows that she will never excel at typing, no matter how many years she types, no matter how hard she tries, no matter how much she can push to motivate herself better. Her reaction is that having reached average competence she will never get any better. Another friend will never learn electrical repairs, because electricity terrifies him. Don't set your sights low, but do not despair if you fail now and again.

Occasionally the best motto is: Some things that are worth doing are worth doing poorly. Deciding just how much is worth learning about a given subject—just how much time, money, and effort you want to invest in it—is one of the most useful judgments to make whenever taking up a new subject. That's why making such an estimate of how important and urgent a project is is one of the initial decisions suggested in the learning plan on page 76. In fact, I would propose setting your sights quite modestly at first, to virtually assure success. A successfully conducted learning project will strengthen your capacity to do more. An overambitious scheme that founders will dispirit you. Think small, and you will build solidly.

Self-exploration is not a process you will ever complete. Maintaining and heightening your awareness of your changing concerns should become a regular part of your learning life, just as your body constantly monitors and feeds back to you information about the state of your physical health. "The person who seeks an education," warns Harold Taylor,

formerly president of Sarah Lawrence College but an educator who is well aware that learning need not take place on
a campus, "must involve himself in discovering the meaning
of his own life and the relation between who he is and what
he might become. Without that vision of a personal future
and a hard look at the reality of one's own situation, the
ultimate purpose of education itself—that is, to grow, to
change, to liberate oneself—is almost impossible to achieve."

Your learning, like your life, will take its shape and draw
its energy from your values and priorities. I have spoken of
learning as a "lever for life-change." The fulcrum of that
lever is this sense of yourself—who you are, what you need
and want, what you seek to become. It is this self-concept
that gives meaning to everything you learn.

This is why so much of conventional higher education
is wasted. Only when students awaken to a sense of themselves and their personal destinies do the riches available
on the campus really become food for thought. Merely making students trek through surveys of this and that or con-
centrate in one subject or another does not add a cubit to
their mental stature. Paradoxically, the people who get the
most out of attending college are usually those who have
already developed such a compelling motivation to learn
that they would probably educate themselves if they had
to. The people who are there to be "given" their education
don't get as much out of the experience. The secret of successful education lies not in the richness of the "offerings"
but in the state of mind of the student.

Your Learning Log

The most important tool of free learning is a log—or
journal, diary, notebook, whatever you choose to call it.
Always have a pad and pencil on hand for jotting down
ideas, thoughts, feelings, and even dreams. (It's also useful
for keeping track of reminders and random information.)

You could talk into a tape recorder as a first step. The

simple process of setting ideas and impressions down—even in a letter, say—usually sharpens them and often prompts us to enlarge and augment them.

The purpose of the log (by whatever name or medium) is to help you keep track of those aspects of your learning and growth that seem most exciting.

Express your ideas, insights, reactions, reflections, problems, and doubts. Also use the log to record your reading, viewing, listening, and interviewing. Later on it may be a useful place to project your plans, dreams, aspirations, and experiments. The log naturally focuses on whatever kind of learning most interests you. For one person it may deal largely with occupational matters, for another it could probe into the unconscious.

Through this basic tool of free learning you will become increasingly conscious of what your daily experiences mean. You will be better able to see patterns in your growth that you might otherwise miss. You will heighten your awareness of your own learning process—what works for you and what doesn't, and why. When you hit a plateau, reviewing the past month's journal entries will help refocus your self-education most effectively.

The journal will also enable you to keep track of those sudden illuminations that will come often, if you expect and welcome them, and that connect one subject with another, or suggest leads to other topics you might want to pursue. Each learning project tends to throw off such sparks.

Think of your learning log in part as an idea bank—a place to store ideas you can't use at the moment but which are too good to forget. Not only does such record keeping enhance and expand your creative powers, it will help you connect facts, perceptions, and ideas, and perhaps lead you up to new and even more satisfying adventures in learning.

Gradually you will begin to discern the longer trajectory of your own learning. You will feel the persistent tug of certain concerns to which your mind especially resonates.

Out of this awareness you will slowly sense the distinctive thrust of your personal adventure of the mind.

Some people have advocated that this be made a conscious choice, early on. "Begin at once [not today or tomorrow or at some remote indefinite date, but right now, at this precise moment]," the pioneering publisher Max Schuster used to tell young people years ago, "to choose some subject, some concept, some great name or idea or event in history on which you can eventually make yourself the world's supreme expert."

Similar advice is offered by Russell Mawby, president of the Kellogg Foundation, who urges "a comprehensive approach to building an individual plan for lifelong learning and growth. Such a plan should reflect the latest concepts of the stages of adult development [and] incorporate . . . personal values and goals."

If this bold advice fits your personal style, more power to you. You will have a handsome head start on pursuing your own intellectual goals. But if it seems too much to manage right now, don't worry. There's a less dramatic way to get the same results.

Just be alert to the gradual build-up of your awareness and commitment to certain basic issues or areas. Take note of the continuities and connections among your various interests. Occasionally reflect on where you seem to be headed intellectually, and how you might strengthen and accelerate your natural movement in that direction. You will find that without strain (though not without some effort and attention) your learning will begin to come into sharper focus.

Most accomplished thinkers keep such a log of their learning. An admittedly extraordinary example is provided by these few entries from the 1958 log of Eric Hoffer, West Coast longshoreman turned writer and pundit, published under the title *Working and Thinking on the Waterfront* (Harper & Row, 1969). They indicate how wide a range of thoughts a day's occupation may provide:

April 15

Eight hours on the *Keito Maru*. A surprisingly easy day, yet in the evening I felt dejected. It is so easy to be dissatisfied with myself. The least transgression weighs on me. To preserve my sense of well being I must lean backward in my dealings with others. A sensitive conscience is probably a symptom of old age. I must be scrupulously decent not in order to feel noble but to feel well.

The lack of enterprise and venturesomeness in the British business world is not easy to explain. High taxes and excessive red tape are not the reason. From my talks with the mates on Swedish ships I gather that taxes and red tape are as high and excessive in Sweden, if not more so. Yet businessmen in Sweden are alert and on the go, and the rate of growth of the Swedish economy is satisfactory. Actually the fact that net profits remain moderate, no matter what, should promote risk taking. You need not worry about the profits. It is not true that people will exert themselves in business only for money. There are other prizes—power, fame, adventure, and sheer achievement. For a game-playing nation like the British, business played as a game should not seem outlandish. What we have, then, in Britain is a lack of exuberance and inner pressure. Do the old in Britain hang on longer to positions of power? Yet, in Japan, too, the old are not discarded. Many of the Japanese tycoons look ancient. My hunch is that the prevailing ideal of the gentlemanly squire makes for leisureliness, understatement and gracious living. Go-getting is vulgar. The British have not won many trophies in sports. The old Samurai tycoons transact business as if they were going to war.

April 16

Nine hours on the *C. E. Dant* at Pier 17. A weary day. Had Skeets for a partner—a poor worker with a bleating voice.

At intervals I peeked into an English translation of the *Lun Yu*. The aphorisms do not seem brilliant, yet you want to reread them. Perhaps it is because of the vagueness of some of the terms, the strangeness of the setting, and even the modernity of some of the sayings. "It is hard to find a man who will study for three years without thinking of a post in government." This is true even now in Asia, Africa, and Latin America. "To remain unconcerned though others do now know of use—that is to be a great man."

April 17

Eight hours on the *C. E. Dant.* Finished the job. Had a new partner, a Negro, very conscientious and nice to be with.

Something I read in the *Manchester Guardian* Weekly started me thinking about the attitude of the masses toward the intellectuals. There is no doubt that to most Portuguese and Italian longshoremen a schoolmaster is an important person, almost as much a dignity as the priest. But through most of history the common people resented the educated as exploiters and oppressors. Rabbi Akiba, who started life as a roustabout, recalled how he used to cry out: "Give me one of the learned and I shall bite him like a jackass." During the peasant uprisings the clerks were given short shrift by the mobs. When in the fourteenth century the mob burned the charters and manuscripts of the University of Cambridge an old hag tossed the ashes into the wind crying: "Away with the learning of the clerks, away with it."

A learning log need not focus on books and ideas. It can also be a personal exploration of one's emotional "inner space." John Robben, a businessman from Connecticut, used such a journal to teach himself some truths about his own life. "It all started to happen two years ago, as I was approaching my fortieth birthday," Robben explains in *Coming to My Senses* (T. Y. Crowell, 1973). "I started to become aware that the way I was living my life—although it wasn't a bad life—wasn't everything it could be. I didn't know exactly what, if anything, could be done about this, but I did know that in spite of many good reasons for living, I couldn't see much value in it."

Pretty much par for the course for an upper-middle-class salesman who commutes to Manhattan every morning. What was extraordinary, however, was John Robben's response to this familiar situation. Instead of bolting, plunging into depression, having an affair, or rushing onto the therapist's couch, Robben adventured into himself. He started exploring—through observation of himself, introspection, experimentation in his daily personal relations, and the traditional power tool of self-discovery, the honest journal—an exploration of the roots of his malaise.

"I believe the only way I can grow as a person is to be as honest about myself and my life as it's possible for me to be," he begins his journal. "Until I say out loud what I feel and think and fantasize about, I really won't know who I am and who lives in me."

The subject matter of Robben's free learning—feeling more honestly, acting more autonomously—is not usually thought of as part of education at all. Here in a representative incident he confronts a kind of irritation most of us have felt:

I'm becoming aware how frequently my family, my friends and my job upset me. . . .

Asking myself *what* I'm feeling instead of why helps me to get more in touch with my feelings. Asking why has the opposite result. When I ask why, my feelings get pushed aside; my concentration falls on external conditions and I become accusatory. I begin to blame the weather, my wife, my job, a head cold, for my irritation.

I must remember to assume responsibility for my feelings. If I'm irritated it's not because Margie didn't make my breakfast, or because my daughter Janet was taking a noisy shower when I was trying to go to sleep, or because my job forces me to come into a hot city and then bores me when I get there. If I'm irritated it's because *I'm* irritating me. . . .

This morning, for example, I had this terribly hemmed-in feeling. I'd given my entire weekend to my family, and now we were being invited to go for a walk at the arboretum with some of our friends. I didn't want to go, but felt obliged to.

"I haven't had a free moment to myself since coming home from work on Friday night," I said to Margie. My voice sounded weak and tired.

"It's your own fault," she said.

"My fault? You're the one who set up all these engagements."

"You don't have to go for the walk. No one's forcing you."

"But you want me to go."

"Sure! But not against your will. Take responsibility for your-self."

"OK," I said, in a strengthening voice. "I'm responsible for not providing myself with a free moment since Friday night."

Immediately I felt capable of doing something about it.

"Taking responsibility," Barry Stevens says, "returns my power to where it belongs—with me."

"I'm not going," I announced.

"Fine," Margie said. "Then we'll go without you."

Taking responsibility returned my power, and I was then able not only to recognize my preference but also to act on it. How simply it happened! When I go along with what others want and deny the reality of my feelings, what others want seems to become my prison, whereas the real prison is in ignoring my feelings. I cannot alter what others want, but I don't have to go along with it. When I do, and then feel frustrated, angry, thwarted, frightened or captured, it's because I've delivered myself up to capacity. No one holds me against my will—unless I deed this privilege to him.

The titles of other sections in Robben's journal give a glimpse of the rest of the "curriculum" he pursued through this kind of learning through consciousness raising, intro-spective analysis, and action testing: "Letting Others Know Where I Am," "Confessing Fears," "Shoulds and Oughts," "Compliments," "Victimized," and "Questions Disguise Un-expressed Needs."

At the end of his book—one assumes it certainly is not the end of his journey of self-discovery and self-affirmation —Robben reflects on the role of this new kind of learning in many people's lives:

The more we find out about ourselves, the more we learn there is to discover. We are not as simple as we formerly be-lieved. Neither are we as satisfied. Going to work and attending church services, and raising children, and living with our spouses, and relating to friends, are not things we take for granted any more. There isn't just one way our cultural training led us to accept doing these things; and until we experiment and try some of the options available to us, we're going to remain victims of our past, imprisoned by the rigidities we were brought up believing in.

Whether your own journal is literary like Eric Hoffer's or introspective like John Robben's, eventually it will become a portfolio of both the processes and the products of your adventures in learning. Its chief value is to you, but it could count heavily should you seek credits or a degree for your free learning, or should a potential employer require evidence of your learning. The journal-portfolio is the free learner's counterpart to the conventional student's transcript of courses taken and grades received.

Planning Your Learning Projects

Heightened awareness of how you keep changing leads naturally to the next phase of this learning business: choosing things to learn, and then figuring the best ways to learn them. Chances are you already have in mind half a dozen things you would like to learn to do or to understand better. I've found that such initial goals should be modest. Anything achieved with ease builds up confidence.

Perhaps you've been meaning to get straight, once and for all, how to judge the comparative value of mutual funds. Or you might like to know how to troubleshoot your fuse box when the lights go out or how to clean and change the spark plugs in your car engine. Again, you might have grown curious about a writer your friends talk about whose work you've never sampled. Or perhaps there's some operation in your office that you'd dismissed as irrelevant to your work but that now looms as something you should understand to improve your performance.

Though these may seem modest exercises, they can be good trial runs for larger adventures. Through such small starts you'll find out how to *make* a start, how to follow through, how to fit deliberate learning into your life. Projects such as these will yield insights into how to pick subjects and methods, what kinds of problems tend to arise, and how you react to them. You will be especially aware of these things if, as I strongly recommend, you log your experiences.

Each venture emboldens you for more learning. And since they all should bring you joy or profit or both, you are getting your rewards at the same time.

A little sensible planning enhances the ease, pleasure, and effect of free learning. Today's environment—the flood of books, magazines, audiovisual materials, and program offerings from numerous agencies and knowledgeable people—creates a bewildering smorgasbord for free learners.

By taking time to scout the possibilities in a given field, you can save money, time, effort, and anguish. Another reason for planning is to ensure as best you can that the changes you intend will be for the best. Let's face it: Change may leave you worse than you were before. "Change" is not identical with positive growth. One of the clichés of our time, neatly punctured by writer Sara Sanborn, is "to call all of the adult changes 'growth,' with the implication of an almost inevitable happy conclusion if we will but yield to the process. This optimism seems to me unjustified by anything except the magic word, 'growth.' Might not some changes represent a Great Leap Sideways? Might not we emerge from some crises not better or worse, but merely different? And even if we hold ourselves ever ready for 'renewal,' might not the world have other plans for us?"

Indeed. In fact, virtually all of us are surrounded by individuals and institutions pressuring us to meet their expectations. Unless you have determined your own needs, it's almost impossible to resist these pressures. The issue is: Their plans, or yours? By setting your own plans for how and why you want to change, you can more effectively direct the shape of your life and make active learning an integral part of it.

For you the most convenient, enjoyable, and effective way to learn something may include a course or part of a course; a book, books, or parts of books; interviews; fact finding at the library; watching selected TV programs; doing volunteer work; making a telephone survey—whatever. The only criteria are:

1. Does it advance your purpose?
2. Is it fun?
3. Is it economical (in both money and time)?
4. Is it preferable to other available choices?

Sometimes planning a learning project may take only five minutes, because the options are obvious or dictated by circumstances. More often, however, the very exercise of planning will reveal choices and possibilities that would not otherwise have occurred to you. The experience of free learners I know indicates that time spent on making smart choices at the start pays for itself in the long run.

Here's a checklist of questions to ask yourself:

Learning Project Plan

_____
(title)

What, exactly, do I want to learn, understand, know about, become, be able to do?

1. How and where can this best be learned? What resources would be useful?
2. When is the best time to learn it, and what would be a desirable schedule and deadline?
3. Who could help?

4. How much is it worth to me? How much will it cost—in time, energy, and money—through various means?
5. How will I know I've achieved the goal, and what documentation or product would be useful to have?

How *much* do I want to learn this? How does it relate to my broader goals right now? How important, and how urgent, is it to me?

If you feel that some friendly help might be useful, it's increasingly at hand. "Learning counseling" is a rapidly emerging field offering advice, information, and aid to adult learners. Learning counselors go by many names and are found in different settings, so you'll have to do a little poking around and keep your eyes open. In Chapter 5, on "The Invisible University," I describe the major ones, such as "learner's advisers" in libraries who can help you plan and conduct your own projects (see page 96), and educational brokers who are expert at matching your needs with programs offered in your area (see page 155). Many college programs designed especially for adults (see page 151) will give you help in clarifying your educational needs and goals as part of their recruitment process. (But you've got to be careful here, for of course they will have a vested interest in signing you up for their programs.) Sometimes all you need is a sympathetic, knowledgeable individual—ideally, one who has himself been through the process. A good nationwide listing of such people is available from Campus-Free College, 1239 G Street N.W., Washington, D.C., 20005.

Creating Your Invisible University

Don't panic. You won't need bricks and mortar to build your own "Invisible University." You won't have to negotiate with a faculty union or get accredited. This university isn't a place but rather your key to existing places. It isn't an organization but an ever growing network of people you'll find useful or fun to learn from or with. It isn't a collection of books but rather an inventory of printed and other kinds of media from which you will want to draw from time to time.

Once you've set up the simple mechanism described below, your university will grow as you become aware of new opportunities and resources. Basically, I'm proposing a free learner's college catalog. But instead of being confined to the resources (and constrained by the requirements) of a single campus, your catalog will be the key to the wealth of possibilities inside and outside campuses.

This invisible university is simply a collection of the most interesting listings, leads, contacts, and other educational things pertinent to your own interests and needs. One section will consist of the catalogs of appropriate sections of your local college's bulletins, another might be a file of bibliographies in your main fields of interest, another of the many informative commercial catalogs, another of people and organizations specializing in your particular interests. Still another file could house relevant ads, newspaper clippings, and other items.

Chapter 5 describes the components of the "Invisible University." From those components, you will pick and choose your own set of resource guides.

But here it might be useful if I briefly described my own "invisible university," a "College in My Head" through which I am currently conducting my own ongoing education.

"The College in My Head" isn't really there, of course— only the central administration is. The college itself is all around me. The local library is one important part of it, but so is my television set. Though books are important, so is the telephone, particularly on topics requiring up-to-dateness.

The faculty of my college includes some experts of national repute, but I meet them through the media rather than in class. The student body is highly congenial; it consists of friends and colleagues who are continuing their own education in fields of interest akin to mine. The campus can be anywhere. I've convened impromptu seminars aboard planes, taken ad hoc tutorials on a commuter train, pursued points by correspondence and phone during the workday, attended symposia via cassettes while soaking in the tub.

My course of study grows out of my needs, enthusiasms, ambitions, and concerns. Sometimes I study a single subject intensively. Such subjects have included choosing stocks, the ecology of a little grove hard by a rented summer cottage in Connecticut, the poetry of Yeats, cooking, copy editing, and new ways to promote personal growth.

At other times I may carry on studies in five or six subjects at once. Among my "minors" over the past two years have been Speedwriting, the causes of inflation, second careers, general semantics, techniques of life planning, popular culture, and humanism.

I pursued each of these in a different way. For example, to master Speedwriting took practice with a handbook and a record. To try to understand inflation I read three books and the relevant sections in two standard college texts and kept my eye peeled for good material in newspapers and magazines, and on television and radio. I learned about second careers primarily through interviews and correspondence, having discovered that the two books on the subject, although only a couple of years old, were already dated because economic conditions and people's attitudes had changed so rapidly. For general semantics I borrowed, through my local library, a set of ten films by S. I. Hayakawa, joined a local group, and subscribed to *ETC*, the lively journal of the movement.

Obviously, my major use of these techniques has been in learning about free learning itself while I was writing this book. These pages distill my five-year log of free learning, the record of some ninety learning projects, large and small, in which I defined what I needed to know next, looked into different ways of getting the facts or help I needed, chose the most convenient and congenial one, did the work (reading, interviewing, analysis, research, whatever), figured out if I had what I needed, and if not what to do about it. The modes of learning I used have included almost all those that compose the "Invisible University"—libraries, colleges, media of all kinds, people ranging from specialized experts to casual acquaintances, organizations and institutions, networks, a learning exchange, and small groups interested in the subject.

My family too seems to have benefited from this more active quest for learning in our home. Often they have joined in my learning projects, and the results have been some lovely mini-seminars in which our two children, ages ten and thirteen, participate more eagerly than they do their school homework. A TV program, a magazine article, a letter or visit from someone interested in something we're interested in, a film or tape I bring home from the library—any of these can start us off on a discussion.

I've been amazed at how quickly and well the kids catch on to things in one of those discussions. I'm also delighted with their growing awareness that learning is something that can go on anywhere, any time, rather than just what happens in school, with a teacher. This may well be more important than any particular thing they learn, because through it they are getting into the habit of being curious, analytical, and creative on their own.

Needless to say, I can always go back to the classroom if it becomes an attractive option—if it can compete, as a mode of learning something I really want to learn, with the economy and convenience of the college in my head. I could even get credit and a degree if I want by taking some of the new tests offered by the New York State Education Department under its Credit-by-Examination and Regents External Degree program.

But in my own case the motivation is the pleasure and usefulness of the things I'm learning. I have a gratifying sense of growth. As my exploration of a subject, topic, or skill deepens, I find I can make subtler distinctions within it, combine parts of it with others or with other fields, define more precisely how I want to proceed. My learning in each field seems to cumulate, continually buoying me just a little higher than when I started out. This sense of gradual but definite advancement toward goals important to me is quietly satisfying.

"But Have I Really Learned?"

How do you know how much or how well you've learned? And how can you provide evidence of what you've learned to other people, if that should be desirable or necessary for a job, to get into college or graduate school, or for other reasons?

There are more answers to this question than most of us think of from our school memories of testing and grading. There are all kinds of ways you can evaluate, assess, judge, and document your free learning. And these ways are more interesting and more useful to your further learning than school-type tests.

Can you delude yourself into thinking you have learned when in fact you haven't? Sure. This has been going on in schools and colleges as long as they have existed. But free learners have some advantages when it comes to evaluation. In a college class you can sit through thirty hours of lectures and for one reason or another—a dreary teacher, a lack of aptitude, insufficient motivation—learn nothing that will last beyond the final exam. Many of my college friends cite courses they passed, often with good grades, which they might as well have skipped for all they learned. (Usually they were reluctant to admit this at the time.) Those thirty or even three hundred hours in the classroom and that B or C grade can truly delude you that you have learned calculus, for instance, or how to speak French.

So forget school and college stereotypes. Don't identify evaluating your learning with the unpleasantness of taking a test and being given a grade. That is *not* the right way to take the measure of learning. Even colleges realize this and are trying to move away from it. They know that if learning is geared to answering examination questions, the student only has to come up with a right answer once, in perhaps one hour of one day, and that this can result in a rate of forgetting that is astonishing and dispiriting. Colleges are rapidly shifting in the direction of "competency-based" credentialing, in which the award of a diploma is based not on the simple piling up of course credits but on demonstrating competence to do specific things. (Free learners therefore are finding it increasingly easier to solicit expert testimony, the judgment of a committee of qualified practitioners, or other evaluation of their learning and achievement.)

Just consider how we find out in everyday life whether someone has certain skills, knowledge, or ability. We ask questions like Can you do this? How well? Who can tell me how you perform in a given situation? Can you follow what I'm doing or talking about? Do you have a license to do this? How much money did you make in this field? Can I see what you've produced? What have you published? What do people in the field say about your work? How do you rank yourself among others whose work you admire?

To get a fresh perspective on how a free learner might evaluate his learning, let's glance back at the people profiled in Chapter 2 and consider some of the ways they evaluated how much or how well they learned.

Cornelius Hirschberg, the salesman who roamed through the great books, compared his reading with a long list of subjects and books that he felt he ought to know. He gauged his accomplishment by looking over his collection of books—a visible expression of his mental university—and contemplating how his familiarity with particular books lasted over time.

Ted Marchi, the road builder, measured his learning by actual accomplishment on the job.

Marvin Weisbord, the businessman who transformed his

company, used his employees' productivity as his "bottom line," while Norman Macbeth, who refuted Darwin, knew that his learning was valid and useful when he got his book published and the reviews were favorable.

Nicholas France, who read his way to a B.A., passed the New York State Regents tests. Tillie Lewis found out that she'd learned to grow tomatoes when her first crop came in; she knew that she had learned how to run a business when the profits piled up.

Michael Rossman, who made his own music, and John Robben, who discovered he marched to a different emotional drummer, both found that if they listened they could hear the harmonies they were making or failing to make.

Helen Baker, the schoolyard lawyer, knew that the results she achieved for her clients depended on the quality of her study and could measure her accomplishment by the number of people she had helped, or failed to, and by the number of cases she had won or lost.

Barbara Andrus appraised her work by the success of the people she trained through her handbook.

Malcolm X felt the consequences of his learning in the strengthened conviction and commitment of his own life and in the powerful influence he exerted on other people as they were moved by him.

These free learners measured their learning by standards growing out of the learning itself, and their lives. For some the measure was a tangible product, like a salable tomato, a usable road, a smoothly running office, or a well-received book. For others it was less tangible but equally important: a new awareness of options in everyday life, a sense of community, a capacity to enrich one's life. For still others it was the change wrought in other people's lives: a child awakened to learning, a parent emboldened to challenge school authorities.

Accomplishments, capabilities, social effects, strengthened sensitivities and convictions—in such consequences is free learning properly measured. Appraising such outcomes is, in a way, more difficult than taking a test at the end of a course and getting a grade. But the rewards are worth the challenge. And this kind of measuring encourages and aids *further* learning.

Here, for example, is how Lynn Hinkle, a commercial artist from Minneapolis, handles the problem:

I've had considerable experience with different aspects of commercial art, but no formal training in a vocational program. What I have been doing and intend to continue doing for credentials is four-fold.

(1) Maintain a complete portfolio of material I have produced.
(2) Describe the particular tasks I undertook for production of the material, like copy writing, graphic design, key-line, and paste-up.
(3) Describe the speed at which I was able to perform these particular tasks that require methodical care with others that can be done more quickly.
(4) List either co-workers or employees who can verify my portfolio and description of my abilities.

If I continue to specify and document my work experience in this manner, I will probably be able to provide as accurate a description of my skills as a commercial artist as someone who can specify the content of certification from a commercial art training program. Although I'm reluctant to speak for anyone else, this knowledge can help me to:

(1) Remind myself of my limitations if I decide to work independently.
(2) Develop a program to learn from or teach the people I work with.
(3) Negotiate with a boss if I decide to work for someone else.

Lynn's listing of specific skills is right in line with what employers are increasingly looking for. Sophisticated career counselors like John Crystal (see page 175) are now advising their clients to forget about the conventional resume.

They advocate just this kind of analysis of one's "skill clusters" to present to prospective employers. As the college degree continues to lose its value as a guarantee of competence, more and more jobs are opening up to people who can show what they know and what they can do.

Note too that in keeping careful track of what she has actually done and produced, Lynn is also making herself aware of what she might want to learn next. I like this kind of appraisal, which feeds back into the learning process. To my mind, one of the most important reasons for evaluating one's learning is to become alert to how one learns, in order to increase the ease and effectiveness of the process.

Chapter 5 / THE INVISIBLE UNIVERSITY

Not I but the city teaches.

—SOCRATES

By the "Invisible University" I mean the wealth of resources and opportunities available to the free learner. These ways to learn and grow range from small grass-roots groups in the women's movement, through "learning exchanges" serving whole communities, to major national projects. The Invisible University includes libraries, museums, films, television, and organizations (social, professional, religious, commercial) that offer opportunities to learn on a more flexible, freer basis than colleges and universities usually do.

Some free learners find this inventory a little intimidating at first. It seems like too much to take account of, to choose from, to organize. One of them compared it to being handed a road map of all the highways in the United States when all you'd asked for was some advice on a nice spot to take your vacation.

Fear not. There's no need to absorb everything that follows. As the New York *Times* says about itself, "You don't have to read it all, but it's nice to know it's all there." Your own needs at any given moment may require only one of these ways to learn, or at most you may need to select a comfortable two or three. But you should always have a varied repertoire; the more options you have, the more likely you'll be to find the one that best suits your particular situation.

The Invisible University

Inexpensive ways to learn in your community. You can comparison-shop for learning opportunities and find what you need cheaply and conveniently.

Libraries. There are new services most people don't know about, like learner's advisers.

Learning exchanges. Find or start this simple agency through which anyone can learn, teach, or both.

Networks. You can plug into one of these invisible networks of people learning from one another on a regular basis via the mails, phone, and inexpensive newsletters.

Learning groups. Convening your own group of co-learners is easier than you think.

Television. Learn economics from John Kenneth Galbraith, art from Kenneth Clark, etc.

Churches. These are beehives of free or inexpensive learning options.

Growth centers. Virtually every community now has places where you can explore yourself, your emotions, and your relationships with other people.

Arts centers. The arts, an ideal way to learn and grow for adults, are burgeoning nationwide.

Generally speaking, this "university" lets you start whenever you want, and learn at your own pace, backtracking and reviewing as much as you like, even changing direction on short notice. You are free to combine resources from different institutions and augment any particular offering with others. You determine the amount of time (and money) to be spent, and measure yourself against your own stan-

Do-it-yourself colleges. Free universities and other forms of do-it-yourself higher education are available widely.

The campus connection. A campus is good for much more than paying your money to take a course.

Correspondence study. More possibilities here than most people imagine. Would you believe Zen, women's lib, French cooking?

Tape cassettes. There's a whole "cassette curriculum" that covers the entire range of college subjects, and much more.

New "open" programs at colleges. You can create your own curriculum, study in your own way (instead of attending classes), and get credits and a degree.

Educational brokers. A whole new profession has emerged just to serve learners.

Games. Through simulation, learn to run a business—or a city.

Activist groups. Learn how society works by trying to change it.

Other resources. Each free learner eventually adds to the Invisible University discoveries of the best ways for him or her to learn from people, organizations, and media.

---

dards. The form of your education is determined by the shape of your unique needs and personality.

Each of us finds his own style: while one fortunate free learner may find a well-stocked library (see page 93), and local learning exchange at hand (see page 99), another might choose listening to a tape cassette series (see page 146), take a national TV course (see page 112), and rent two or three outstanding films. A third learner might elect a university correspondence course (see page 143), join (or organize) a discussion group (see page 107), and obtain credits toward a degree by examination (see page 158). Still another might turn to a community action project to study who gets what, where, and how.

DISCOVERING LEARNING OPPORTUNITIES IN YOUR COMMUNITY

Every community of any size contains myriad opportunities, resources, and possibilities for free learning. Finding them is largely a matter of keeping your eyes open as you go about your daily business. Talk to bright people, look for notices in local publications, store windows, or on bulletin boards.

In large cities the opportunities are almost limitless. Students from the New School for Social Research, in New York City, went out into the streets around their school and found over one hundred resources for learning within a five-block radius: dance and music studios, social action organizations, church programs, storefront training centers, craftsmen and shopowners willing and eager to teach, a chess club and sensitivity groups, among others. A St. Louis friend talked to a knowledgeable neighbor and within an hour had a list of over thirty kinds of opportunities, some organized, some informal, and all close to home. They ranged from French lessons to theater workshops, poetry readings, and a group of artists who met together weekly to sketch.

Local newspapers provide excellent leads for free learners —articles about lectures, concerts, classes; they also carry advertisements for all sorts of groups. Regional publications —*New Orleans, Chicago, New York, Vermont Life, New West, Sunset,* to name a few—publish calendars of events, vignettes about interesting activities, and articles about opportunities for all kinds of learning.

Of course there are also the bulletin boards in your neighborhood—at the library, the supermarket, school, laundromat, church, bookstore. "Interested in Learning Spanish?", "Piano Instruction," "Study with Photographer," "Beginners' Tennis Group Every Saturday Morning"—what you want to learn may be available for the asking in your own back yard.

While searching, keep in mind that the most advantageous tool is a catalog or directory of learning opportunities in your community—if one exists. In Minneapolis the *Vocational Skills Training Director* was compiled by the New Vocations Project; it sells for one dollar. Over fifty pages of listings include private vocational schools and technical institutes, programs offered through the public schools, apprenticeship programs, correspondence schools in the state, places to explore skills, and counseling services.

Thanks to this fine tool, Minneapolitans have laid out for them the alternative ways they can study whatever it is they want to learn. If one wants to train to be a keypunch operator, for example, there are seven entries to investigate, including both public and private schools, and both classroom and correspondence options. If one wants to become a nurse, there are over twenty different places to write to. In less familiar fields there are fewer listings, but usually some: two institutions offer training to become a quality control technician, for instance; two offer courses in merchandising display; three offer landscape design.

Unfortunately in most communities no one takes the trouble to organize such lists. However, you yourself could decide to assemble the available information, and it would be an excellent learning experience. If you do so, also find an institution that agrees to be a central repository for the information—perhaps a library, a school, or a college.

The recent experience of my friend Janice Hapgood illustrates the advantages of comparison shopping. Instead of just signing up at one of the highly visible universities in downtown Manhattan, she took the time to find out about other opportunities. Sure enough, she discovered that conversational French cost $100 or more per semester for a class with at least twenty other students at the local universities. At the Alliance Française, a seven-week class with only eight students cost thirty-five dollars, with authentic French instructors, varied teaching materials, and a charming townhouse instead of a sterile classroom.

Janice also wanted to study painting, and here again she found a bargain—and an experience surpassing that of the usual course. She found that practicing artists taught painting in the neighborhood public high school as part of the New York City schools' adult education program. The cost was much less than at any college or art school in the city—thirty-five dollars for ten two-hour sessions—and the instructor was "marvelous."

"Aside from saving money, I think I learned more," Janice says. "The teachers worked hard because the classes were serious and obviously important to the students. No one showed up unprepared, because you might be the only one there that day! So before I ever sign up for another course, I will ask around, do some research over the telephone, and talk to people who know the field I'm interested in."

Bicycle repair was on one friend's list of projects. At the American Youth Hostel headquarters she got four two-hour classes for twelve dollars, and the class was held in a loft.

In each of these cases the students found the ambience more to their taste than it would have been in more conventional classes. One convert says, "There was much more diversity in age, sex, race, and economic status than in regular college classes. The age range, for instance, was always from the late teens right up into the eighties—even for bicycle repair!"

In large cities you may find that a composite listing of all courses offered by all institutions is available each term. In Boston, for example, a listing is offered by the Educational

Exchange, and in New York City such information is provided by phone as well as in printed form by the Regional Center for Lifelong Learning.

Private trade and technical schools are also well worth investigation. Despite the unsavory reputation given them by some unscrupulous operators, most such schools do deliver what they promise—relevant vocational training at reasonable cost. *Getting Skilled* by Tom Hebert and John Coyne (Dutton, 1976) is an irreverent but careful study and listing of accredited schools; it also samples non-accredited ones. (You might also want to check out the same authors' *By Hand: A Guide to Schools and Careers in Crafts* [Dutton, 1975].)

A comprehensive sourcebook to occupations that don't require a college degree is *The Guide To Career Education* by Muriel Lederer (Quadrangle Books, 1975). It describes 200 lines of work (with a promise to expand in the next few years) and indicates for each one what aptitudes and abilities are needed, what education or training is required, the salary range and opportunities for advancement, and how to get further information. Listed are not only apprenticeships but also community-college programs, training in industry, cooperative education (work-study) programs, and government-sponsored programs.

USING INNOVATIVE LIBRARY SERVICES*

The library has always been the second home of free learners. Here they have traditionally found exactly what they want, when they want it, without the bureaucratic hassles and heavy costs that encumber formal education.

Nowadays libraries have even more to offer than ever before. They can often serve free learners in unexpected

---

* This section is the work of Joseph Covino, director of the Great Neck Library, and a leader in making libraries more responsive to the needs of lifelong learners.

and useful ways that most people haven't heard of and only a handful know how to use. Such aid and comfort is available for the asking.

Central to the library of course is its book collection, which may have special strengths in your field of interest. The card catalog will give you an overall picture of what the library has and will steer you to the right section of the open shelves for the subject at hand. The books on the shelves will in turn, through their bibliographies, suggest other books. By comparing bibliographies on any subject, you are likely to find an easy way to identify the best (or at least the most highly regarded and the most often quoted) works in the field. Books that turn up frequently in bibliographies usually are worth paying attention to.

Reference books abound. Their variety is so dazzling that I've reserved a section for them on page 149.

If you can't find what you're looking for, it doesn't necessarily mean that the library doesn't have it. Ask a librarian for help. By observing what the librarian does—what library tools are used—and asking questions, you might learn new ways to use the library more effectively.

Most libraries have open-shelf magazine and newspaper racks. If language is your thing, there are usually foreign periodicals. There are also hundreds of special interest magazines, for example, about photography, stereo equipment, or automobiles. Ask for a directory of publications to see if you have completely surveyed the field.

In addition to a wide range of music selections, the library's record collection may well contain foreign language recordings, plays, radio documentaries, and poetry readings. Are other media available? Many libraries now routinely circulate films and slides. Some even lend or rent projectors. Some check out tape cassettes (see page 148 for the range you may find). The library may be able to get access on your behalf to larger audiovisual storehouses in the public schools or colleges.

Check the reference department. There are some nifty

reference books for the free learner—directories of organizations by type (*Encyclopedia of Associations, Directory of Research Centers*); vocational information (*Resources: Recommendations for Adult Career Resources Supplement*); and standard reference works, such as yearbooks or guides within your special area of interest, e.g., *The Yearbook of Education.*

Another place to start is *The Whole Earth Catalog* (and its sequel, *The Last Whole Earth Catalog*), a tool made so well that it became a work of art. While many items in the catalog may have been superseded by now (it was last published in 1971), the book itself remains the pioneering attempt to make accessible many learning resources of the Invisible University.

A succession of similar catalogs, some mere imitators and some extremely useful, followed *The Whole Earth Catalog.* One of the best for free learners is *Somewhere Else,* a directory of "places that will let you get your hands dirty and places that will leave you alone to work out the struggle between you and whatever hunk of the world you're grappling with," as the editors put it. The four hundred annotated entries give information on where to go to learn blacksmithing, jewelry making, homesteading, record production, and dome building; where to find books and directories leading to alternate ways of life; where to find people of similar interests; how to go to sea or become an apprentice; where to exchange what you know for what you want to learn. In short, *Somewhere Else* is about people and places and networks and centers and books and groups you might not otherwise hear about—but wish you had.

See if the library has a bulletin or calendar of events listing lectures, discussion groups (Great Books, current affairs, or others), workshops, films, concerts, and so on. If you have young children, find out about story hours or preschool activities. These can provide babysitting services that help your children to learn while you pursue your own learning program.

When you use the library, try to evaluate the professional staff. As in all organizations, there is usually a wide range of competence among the employees. If you are inadequately served by one librarian, don't give up. Try others. Build up a good working relationship with those who are most helpful and most familiar with the library collection. The librarian is a key to the resources of the library; if you locate a skilled librarian who cares, your use of the library will be a pleasure.

If the library does not have the material you are looking for—a book, a magazine, a phonograph record—interlibrary loans may be possible. Libraries in small communities often can, and do, borrow from state or large municipal libraries. In large cities interlibrary loans between branches are common and frequent.

Does your library have a learner's advisory service? This innovation may not yet be available, but asking for it might help speed its arrival. Briefly, the learner's adviser is a librarian who will be your personal learning consultant; he or she has been specially trained to help you articulate your needs and goals, plan a learning program, select and obtain materials, and solve problems in the learning process as they arise. Usually the smartest, most personable, and most committed librarians have involved themselves in the program. If there is a learner's adviser, introduce yourself. You will acquire an invaluable consultant for your learning.

These learner's advisers are much more creative and adventuresome than the usual librarian behind a desk. For example, adviser Edith McCauley in Portland, Maine, helped a patron achieve his goal of owning and operating a small commercial fishing boat. She not only found him the materials he needed to learn about the fishing business, but brought him into contact with a specialist in marine science who taught a workshop in navigation. She also introduced him to a lawyer who had recently left his legal practice to set up a small commercial fishing business.

In West Islip, New York, library adviser Guang Nan Chen aided a thirty-five-year-old homemaker who had majored in psychology before dropping out of college. The woman had developed an interest in Hindu religion and Oriental philosophy. Eventually she wanted to read scriptures in the original Sanskrit; she also wanted to study contemporary schools of transpersonal psychology. Adviser Chen supplemented the woman's personal collection of books, periodicals, and tapes with others, many borrowed from nearby libraries. For Sanskrit, she put the learner in contact with the nearest branch of the Institute for Advanced Studies of World Religions, and with foreign language experts in New York State.

Many libraries are now involved in external degree or degree-by-examination programs. Some offer special facilities and materials and even workshops and counseling to help students in these programs. The Denver Public Library is outstanding in this and is pioneering in areas that other libraries will soon be adopting. The Denver Public Library offers seven distinct "On Your Own" programs constituting "a new comfortable approach to independent learning." The seven areas are:

1. CLEP. A program to earn two years of undergraduate college credit in your own time at your own speed (see page 159).
2. G.E.D. High school equivalency program.
3. Great Books. Reading program to explore the Western world's literature.
4. Right to Read. Program to teach basic reading skills and English as a second language.
5. Self-Directed Learning. Rewarding non-traditional approaches to learning whatever interests you.
6. SURGE. Videotaped postgraduate courses in business and engineering from Colorado State University (CSU credit available).
7. TIMEALIVE! A multimedia individualized program to study times, peoples, and places in the world's history.

The Denver Public Library may be unusual, but you need not settle for mediocre or inadequate library facilities. If a wide range of resources, services, and programs is not available in your library, perhaps you can spur the creation of one or more new things by becoming a library advocate. That's how many of the various library programs got started in the first place. Many librarians thrive on being asked to do new things and quite possibly have been wanting for some time to start just the services or the programs you have in mind. Without evidence or demonstration of public interest in new programs, however, they find it hard to argue for them or to justify them. As an advocate you can discuss the library's inadequacies with the librarian, the library director, and with the library's board of trustees. You can search out others who feel as you do and form a group to press for improved and extended services. With your assistance the library can become the center for truly independent learning that it ought to be.

To find out if there is a library in your community with some kind of advisory program for adult learners, write:

    Adult Independent Learning Project
    Consortium for Public Library Innovation
    Tulsa City County Library
    400 Civic Center
    Tulsa, Oklahoma 74103

New York State residents should write:

    Adult Independent Learners Program
    Higher Education Library Advisory Service
    New York State Library
    Albany, New York 12224
      or
    Regents External Degree Program
    Public Library Postsecondary Education Advisory
      Service
    University of the State of New York
    99 Washington Avenue
    Albany, New York 12210

FINDING PARTNERS THROUGH A
LEARNING EXCHANGE

To help learners find resources, a social invention is popping up all over the country. Learning exchanges are a kind of intellectual dating bureau. Basically, a learning exchange links up people interested in the same thing.

Such services have been established in the past three years in more than forty communities throughout the country and on many campuses. Denis Detzel, creator of metropolitan Chicago's Learning Exchange, in Evanston, Illinois, says, "All you need to start is a telephone and a box of file cards. We started with twenty-five dollars. There were five of us; I was a graduate student in education at Northwestern. I realized that there were hundreds, maybe thousands, in my community who wanted to learn something, and also a lot of people with useful or interesting skills or knowledge that they might be willing to teach. Why not match them up?"

Detzel and friends started by passing out leaflets asking people to simply sign up, free, and indicate what they wanted to teach, learn, or just get together to discuss. The function of the exchange was to put appropriate people in touch with one another. Volunteers took turns manning the telephone in the evening.

Responses were slow at first. "Everybody said it was a great idea," Detzel remembers, "but nobody telephoned." So he and Bob Lewis, his chief co-worker, worked hard to publicize the project through local newspapers and radio stations. They put posters in stores, libraries, and wherever people gathered. Soon business picked up, and the matching up began: a bagpipe band met every week in a church; more than thirty people learned self-defense from a high school student in his family's basement; a clown workshop was held in a YMCA gym (the final exam was a clowning stint in the Christmas parade); a series of workshops took place on maintaining Volkswagens, using the streets and available garages. Besides such unconventional studies, the exchange also matched up people wanting to learn (or teach) earth science, modern European literature, Russian culture, analytical chemistry, and other more strictly academic subjects.

Learning exchanges are open to more members of the whole community than are school or college programs. Minority groups, grade school children and the retired, people with zero years of formal schooling and those with law degrees and Ph.D.'s, the rich and not so rich—all have used the services of this learning exchange.

Eleven-year-old Curtis Borman, for example, was interested in 747s. He checked with the exchange for listings on the subject. He was referred to Jack Parkhurst, representative of Lockheed Aviation in Chicago, who invited Curtis and his family to join him at O'Hare Field for what turned out to be the most thorough tour of jumbo jets ever. In the course of the hour-and-a-half tour, Mr. Parkhurst showed the Bormans the ins and outs of the 747, the DC-10, and Lockheed's 10-11. He also told them about his own background and training and explained his job, which included preventive maintenance, troubleshooting, and emergency repairs. For his special research project at school, Curtis wrote about jumbo jets; his paper rated an "outstanding." His father reports, "His fascination hasn't ended yet either; he's still checking out books on the subject from the library. I learned something too, and in the company of my son, who initiated the whole idea."

"The Learning Exchange is based in part on the principle that people who have skills are capable of teaching them," says John McKnight, chairman of the Learning Exchange's board. "Any urban area is rich with people and resources, and the existing institutions just don't meet the demands. We have found a way to help cut down on the isolation and alienation of people in the community, while at the same time putting wasted resources to good use."

No formal credentials are required of the teachers; more than 3000 people have registered to teach one subject or another. Though at first there was some question about maintaining high teaching standards, 97 percent of the exchange's clients who meet with teachers express satisfaction with the arrangements made. Mr. Detzel explains it this way: "All the parties involved are directly accountable to one another. If a client doesn't like a situation, he simply moves on to another. We've found that either the teachers produce or the learners find other teachers."

Even though the Learning Exchange currently serves over 20,000 people in metropolitan Chicago and employs a staff of six part-time and six full-time people, costs are still low. It also provides education in an atmosphere more congenial, to some people, than a teacher-controlled classroom.

Detzel, who thinks the Learning Exchange is an idea whose time has come, predicts that every major city in the United States will have a comparable organization by the end of the decade. Already there are organizations built on the Chicago model in DeKalb, Illinois; Tacoma, Washington; Ann Arbor, Michigan; Binghamton, New York; and as far away as London and Melbourne.

The learning exchange idea can be applied to special situations and selected segments of the population too. I've initiated ad hoc exchanges at conferences, in classes I've conducted, and within schools and social agencies such as drug centers. An imaginative proposal has been made by "Me," the creator of the newsletter *Observations from the Treadmill,* to link the young and the old for learning. "There are millions of older people who have spent the better part of their lives learning a trade, craft, business, or profession. Now they are retired, and we do nothing with their knowledge. There are millions of high school students who will eventually move into these same trades, crafts, businesses, and professions. They could use that knowledge. Link them up as part of the curriculum in tutorials and seminars held in facilities made available by former employers."

Learning exchanges and community information networks can lead beyond promoting individual growth. Groups can take form out of shared interests discovered through the exchange, often focused on problems and issues facing a community or a certain group within the community. Such dialogues can, in turn, lead to coalition building to effect social change.

This is the pattern—information exchange, community dialogue, coalition building for civic potency—which is being promoted by the National Self-Help Resource Center in Washington, D.C. Developed and endorsed by a task force of thirty-one national women's organizations, it is designed to help people all over the country get together to solve their communities' problems. Community resource centers are being organized around the country to coordinate these activities.

Some Learning Exchanges Around the Country

Binghamton Learning Exchange
P.O. Box 862
Binghamton, New York 13902
Peg Johnston

The De Kalb Learning Exchange
157½ East Lincoln
De Kalb, Illinois 60115
Sue Chase

Free Learning Exchange
526 East 52nd
Indianapolis, Indiana 46205

The Free University Network
615 Fairchild Terrace
Manhattan, Kansas 66506
Sheila Russell

INFO
2600 Pennsylvania Avenue
Wilmington, Delaware 19806
Virginia Gregory

The Learning Exchange
P.O. Box 920
Evanston, Illinois 60204

The Learning Exchange
Guild House
802 Monroe Street
Ann Arbor, Michigan 48104

The Learning Network
1411 University Avenue SE.
Minneapolis, Minnesota 55414
Kate Blau

LINK
c/o Action Studies Program
University of Iowa
Iowa City, Iowa 52242
Jeff Weih

Tacoma Learning Exchange
712 South 14th Street
Tacoma, Washington 98405

PLUGGING INTO A NETWORK

There's another kind of network you can plug into—national in scope and focused on your particular interest. These are informal non-institutionalized webs connecting people interested in a specific subject or a particular issue or problem who are willing to share their excitement, insights, methods, and understanding.

Some of these networks number ten people, others thousands. The subjects or concerns that bring them together range from butterflies and chess to the geology of the Rocky Mountains and Shakespeare's tragedies. The most advanced networks link scholars and scientists working on the frontier of a specialty who share their findings by mail months and even years before their work appears in learned journals.

Some communicate wholly by letters. "I live out of the way in Mexico," says Ivan Illich. "I write letters and get them, that's my invisible university." A network of letter writers can provide the basis for an intriguing newsletter like Irv Thomas's *Yin Times,* which aspires, in the editor's words, to "build an inexpensive in-family newsletter into a cross-country sharing of awareness and support."

Other networks have publications ranging from mimeographed newsletters like the *Worm-Runner's Digest,* to informal bimonthlies like *Alternate Sources of Energy,* to journals like *Psychology Today.*

One way to join such a network is to write directly to authors of articles you like; they will be likely to welcome you into their network of correspondence. *Psychology Today,* for example, encourages mini-networks of readers by telling where to write each author or researcher for more information.

Obviously when you join a network you ought to have something to offer and be willing to work at keeping up your end. Since the relationship is completely voluntary, your correspondents have as much right to decline to participate as you have to approach them. Free learning is no free lunch. But most people are generous of spirit when it comes to responding to a newcomer's interest in their field—provided the interest seems informed and courteous.

These networks offer excellent entry points to new areas of knowledge or interest—entry points that are often better than starting with a textbook or introductory course. Except in highly technical fields, it's quite easy for an intelligent newcomer to tune in to what is going on. By doing so, you will find yourself at the exciting frontier rather than mired in the largely outdated "basics" of the subject at hand. And involvement in such a network will probably lead to good ways to master background knowledge if and when really needed. The network may well put you on to local resources —people, events, even really good courses—that would not have come to your attention otherwise.

The "how to" on this one has to be left up to you, because it depends entirely on your particular field of interest. But a typical example of the rapid assimilation into a new field that one can achieve through networking will suggest how to follow up in your own field. Jerry Figgins, a systems analyst from New Jersey, became interested a few years ago in the relation between people's language and their actions when he attended a lecture on general semantics. After the lecture he signed up for the mimeographed newsletter of the New York Society for General Semantics, which brought him news of further lectures, workshops, and publications. Through those listings he was led to the magazine *ETC.*, which publishes research and theory in the field. He caught up on basic readings at the library, and found the names of others interested in the field. Rapidly, Jerry became familiar with the subject, exposing himself to various viewpoints on it and making it part of his intellectual apparatus. Within a year he was beginning to use it in his work. All without any formal study or direct teaching and at minimum cost. "Actually," Jerry reports, "I found that I just absorbed the subject from constant exposure to it without ever having to sit down and really 'study' the books."

No network to be found in your field of interest? Then start one. You can be the hub by beginning a quick-and-dirty—but serviceable—newsletter for the field.

Start off with a single sheet Xeroxed at someone's office, sent to maybe a dozen people. I've seen such sheets sometimes grow astonishingly, in practically any field you can think of: consumerism, model planes, horticulture, *Star Trek,* Sanskrit. That's the way Marshall McLuhan's ideas began wafting down from Canada in the late 1950s: blue dittoed sheets, virtually unreadable, sent to people he'd met at English teachers' conventions.

Usually these newsletters are the expression of one person's interests and commitments, like Irv Thomas's *Yin Times,* Maxine Cushing Gray's *Northwest Arts,* or the utterly idiosyncratic *Observations from the Treadmill* published by "Me."

Out of the proliferation of such self-published network newsletters have come some lasting publications that have achieved a considerable following: I. F. Stone's radical *Weekly,* Henry Geiger's ruminative *Manas,* and John Wilcox's counterculture *Scenes.*

Sometimes too such networks have provided the basis for a lifelong enterprise in sharing one's learning. Lloyd deMause became fascinated by psychohistory, a field that was becoming popular back in the late 1950s when he was a graduate student in political science at Columbia University. He was simultaneously undergoing psychoanalysis and taking advanced courses in psychoanalysis at the National Psychological Association for Psychoanalysis. But deMause discovered that his new preoccupation could not be accommodated by either of the institutions he was attending; his adviser at Columbia said he didn't understand a word deMause had written on his doctoral proposal, and the psychoanalytic institute wanted to work only with people who would see patients. Most students would have found such lack of interest and support on the part of their alma maters sufficiently discouraging to stifle their personal curiosity about a new and risky field. But deMause held fast to his interest.

After figuring out how to make his living, deMause devoted all his spare time to psychohistory. He started the first newsletter in the field, pursued research on his own at the New York Public Library and other collections, and began corresponding with the few psychoanalysts and academics who were experts in the subject. Now, fifteen years later, the field has burgeoned. DeMause's newsletter has become the *Journal of Psychohistory,* his network of collaborative inquirers has generated the two major sourcebooks—*The History of Childhood* and *The New Psychohistory*—and he has started an Institute for Psychohistory, with thirty research associates and regular workshops open to the public, as well as a Psychohistory Press to publish their research results.

One advantage of operating outside the Establishment is being unconstrained by pedantic protocol. "DeMause is no conventional academic," wrote one reviewer of *The History of Childhood,* "but a richly eccentric entrepreneur whose promotional methods are far removed from the staid practices of, say, the *English Historical Review.* The brochures which launched the *History of Childhood Quarterly* depicted a horrifying range of apparatus for the torture and sexual disciplining of children; and a cash prize was offered for the earliest historical example of a child who could be proved *never* to have been beaten."

When the prestigious *New York Review of Books* reviewed deMause's *History of Childhood* volume, the reviewer called him "an academic dropout, a successful businessman and self-taught psychohistorian." This last label amuses deMause, who points out that "since there were no courses in psychohistory when I started, I can hardly avoid being self-taught. I don't mean to compare myself to the master, but it's like calling Freud a self-taught psychoanalyst. Academics don't know quite what to make of me—I've never bothered to get the credentials, the academic position, or the grant funding to do what I'm doing. But I'm finding ways to do it anyway."

As an independent scholar, deMause is not unique. Many of the thirty researchers who are part of his institute are, like him, *not* full-time or even part-time academics, but earn their living in various non-academic ways. And this is only one special field. There are a thousand such areas of inquiry in which a determined individual can, as deMause did, initiate a network of like-minded learners and thereby make a significant contribution to the growth of ideas and knowledge. Or just enjoy being at the center of a gaggle of fellow enthusiasts.

A final thought: You don't even have to commit yourself to an ongoing publication. There's no law against one shots —writing up one's thoughts and distributing them to possibly interested parties. Ron Jones, who does this with teachers in San Francisco, calls it "spontaneous publishing."

"It stems from a person who gets an idea and simply publishes it as a one-time statement and sends it to all of his or her friends," he says. "If a large number of the general public became their own media, the exchange of ideas would be very exciting. We have been trained to be consumers, but what if we became producers."

JOINING OR FORMING A LEARNING GROUP

You can enjoy the benefits of group learning without enrolling in a formal class. Either join or form a learning group dedicated to an interest or goal you share with others. Such informal learning groups usually engender much more *esprit* and participation than do formal classes. They move at the pace and in the direction the participants choose. The whole setup is non-authoritarian. Everyone starts more or less on the same level, and leadership either emerges because it serves the real needs of the group or it soon loses its sway. Moreover, because forming groups is so cheap and easy, mistakes can be quickly rectified; a fresh start is easy to make.

Many groups are already in existence—hobby groups, singles' clubs, women's groups, investors' clubs, growth or encounter groups, and transcendental meditation classes. If you decide to form your own group, you will usually find support and help readily available. For example, to start an investment club you can get basic information and guidance on further reading from major stock exchanges and brokers. They will also be delighted to send you newsletters. Business magazines offer counsel on methods of investing. Financial advisory services and newsletters advertise in the financial pages of major newspapers. They all offer brochures or publications. Individual companies offer brochures on their operations. Home study courses are available. Tools such as stock selection guides and stock comparison charts are available from the National Association of Investment Clubs (NAIC), P.O. Box 220, Royal Oak, Michigan 48068, and other sources. The NAIC will provide encouragement and support to individuals or groups who want to learn to invest soundly. In addition to the national association, many cities have NAIC councils that provide closer-to-home help in starting and running an investment club.

But you can start a group on a subject that doesn't even exist as a "field." I started one several months ago on public interest writing. A group of us who want to use our talents for the public good get together once a month to share ideas, information, and experiences. Guest experts are invited to present their views; so far they've included Deirdre Carmody, who covers the press for *The New York Times;* Christopher Cory, director of public affairs for the Carnegie Council on Children; and Elizabeth Levy, author of *By-lines: Profiles of Investigative Reporters.*

The following tips may serve as a checklist for starting your own group and also may give you the confidence to proceed.

Start by giving your group a name, the simpler the better. An organizational label is apt to make people feel comfortable. (For example, The Free Learning Project was the group that initially helped with this book.)

You may well find enough people interested in the subject among your acquaintances to get started that way. For more members, post notices on various bulletin boards, place an ad, or get a story printed in your local paper.

Where to meet? You can almost always start on a volunteer basis with the homes of those in the group, and then branch out to night use of someone's offices or to a room at the library or a college's student center or a church where space can be reserved.

Some of the best groups I've been in have notably *not* settled down to the subject at hand for the first few sessions. Then when the discussion does finally focus on the topic of the session, everyone's more relaxed and comfortable. A few minutes at the end of each session should be set aside for free-for-all comments about the group and how it's going. In cases where there's an obvious need for change, a committee of about three people, including the person most concerned about the problem, can be appointed to confer before the next meeting to make recommendations.

Depending on the wishes of the group, meetings can take a variety of styles. Probably the more flexibility, the better. Formal leadership may be vested in one person or it may shift to a different person at each meeting or there can be an even less formal plan. Don't worry if discussions range widely and fail to converge at an easily summed up point. The very delight and usefulness of the discussion is in the free flow of thought and feeling. This is the nature of open-ended group learning.

Taking notes is an excellent practice. One person at each session should be responsible for taking notes, typing them up, and, if possible, making copies for everyone before the next meeting. A recorder can liven the notes up with his or her comments and criticisms. However, even a mere list of topics covered, references mentioned, and facts and leads brought up is useful.

All members should try to find learning tools that would interest and help the group—newspaper and magazine articles, tape cassettes or records, films that can be easily borrowed and screened. If members of the group agree to listen beforehand, television and radio shows can be used as topics of discussion.

Books, of course, should be added to this list. The group can work its way through one text (*not* a textbook) that everyone considers important and interesting, although I prefer to use books in pieces. People can read just one section or chapter of the same book, or each individual can read a whole book of his choice on the subject at hand and report on it briefly for use in the discussion. This approach enriches the group with perspectives from many authors.

The community itself may be a resource. A small group can be mobile and flexible, meeting at places that serve its purposes: a museum, a supermarket if you're studying grocery prices, or at a conference being held in your community. Invite local experts to sit in with you from time to time, or ask if the group can meet in the offices of the experts. Experts are more willing to be available than you'd suspect, and will usually be intrigued that a group exists which is interested in their field.

Don't be afraid of changing and/or ending the group when signs appear that the group may have fulfilled its purpose. The members may be ready to "graduate" to other activities. A review of the group's discussions may indicate how to proceed, what changes to make. It's very possible that the group has finished its work and given its members what they could get from this particular configuration of subject, people, time, and place.

Sometimes a learning group will really take off, inventing

its own techniques for achieving its members' purposes. Pamela Allen, co-founder of a women's consciousness-raising group in San Francisco, writes about the unique process they developed. "We have defined our group as a place in which to think," she explains. "A place to think about our lives, our society, and our potential for being creative individuals and for building a women's movement."

The group developed a four-stage "process" for each meeting, or for each unit of work, to help members in their endeavors to become autonomous in their thinking and behavior. "We call these processes opening up, sharing, analyzing, and abstracting. Opening up is our way of keeping in touch with our emotions; through sharing we are giving one another information regarding experiences we have had; in analyzing we are trying to understand the meaning of those events; and finally through abstracting we are fitting that understanding into an overview of our potential as human beings and the reality of our society, i.e., of developing an ideology."

This attempt to structure discussions is just one pattern a group like this might follow, for just as interesting individuals differ greatly, so do the "support groups" such as those in the women's movement. Such groups offer a kind of therapy but usually are not run by therapists. The participants are drawn together by a mutual urge to grow, to know themselves and others better; they want to enliven and strengthen their capacity for relationships with others. This largely neglected aspect of education can be learned in such groups, and it is every bit as valuable as any other kind of learning.

Methods invented by one group can be shared with others of similar focus. In the Marco-Analysis Seminar, developed by a Philadelphia collective, each group begins with issues and problems that are bothering members in their personal lives. But through an interesting method of tracing "webs" of influence and impact, they establish that those problems we think of as personal and individual frequently have roots in the way the society, economy, and government are organized. Through such analysis the participants become aware that the root causes of their problems, and the best hope for relief, lie in "marco" changes in the structure of the economy and the society. The seminar is designed to move the participants to take action for social change based on these insights.

Some social critics see in the proliferation of small groups one of the most heartening signs of renewal in our culture. Erich Fromm writes about them as the building blocks of a "revolution of hope," in a book of that title. Fromm sees small groups as satisfying "the need of the individual to work actively together with others, to talk, plan, and act together, to do something which is meaningful beyond the money-making activities of everyday life. To relate in a less alienated fashion than is customary in most relations to others, to make sacrifices . . . to be open and 'vulnerable,' to be imaginative, to rely on one's own judgment and decision."

CULTIVATING THE TV WASTELAND*

There's plenty of fare for the mind on TV, but it takes a little effort to pluck it out from the flood of pap. Most people, Eric Sevareid has rightly noted, "will make plans, go to trouble and expense, when they buy a book or reserve a seat in a theater. They will not study the week's offerings of music or drama or serious documentation in the radio- and TV-program pages of their newspaper and then schedule themselves to be present. They want to come home, eat dinner, twist the dial, and find something agreeable ready, accommodating to their schedule."

You can make television work for you as a free learner. First of all find out what programs are available and then

---

* This section is by Frederick Breitenfeld, Jr., executive director of the Maryland Center for Public Broadcasting, and a pioneer in harnessing TV to serve learners.

choose them systematically. The Television Information Office, 745 Fifth Avenue, New York, New York 10022, an agency established by the National Association of Broadcasters, previews many of the better TV specials. Its guides for teachers suggest ways to use selected commercial programs in your self-education.

The problem in learning from television, however, is that the medium's offerings lack structure. A talk show last week, a documentary today, a relevant film the day after tomorrow, a panel discussion next month—it doesn't add up, and so it tends to make small impact. There are several ways to inject more structure, purpose, and follow-through into television viewing so that it relates to what you want to learn.

First, use a program or series that has a structure built in. For *The Ascent of Man,* for example, the book by Jacob Bronowski could be used as collateral reading to reinforce the structured sequence of the series itself. For even more structure, it was possible to sign up for a TV correspondence course through local colleges. There is usually one such program or more on public television nowadays. If one suits your purpose, use it.

A second way, more troublesome but worth it if the program meets your special needs, is to build a structure around a program or series yourself. You and several others can meet weekly, view a program, and then discuss it and compare notes, reactions, and thoughts. Basing a listening group on a series like *The Ascent of Man, Wall Street Week,* the *Civilisation* series conducted by Kenneth Clark, or a weekly news analysis, can provide as much stimulation and learning as most college classes, perhaps more.

You can also create an individual learning project in a similar fashion. Let's say you want to improve your buying habits, and a series on consumer economics is announced for the coming week on a local news show. So stop in at the library before the first program and look over the various consumer magazines. See what the librarian can come up with as collateral reading. Try some modest experiments in comparison shopping on your weekly trip to the supermarket and keep careful track of how much you are able to save. (You can select the items first in your usual way, then retrace your steps looking for ways to save.) You may be able to cut off, say, 10 percent of the total amount.

During the week, as the series progresses, talk about the series with people you meet. You may find someone with an especially enlightening experience in such matters. Visit a bookstore and take a look at the proven guidebooks among the paperbacks as well as new publications in the field. Follow up any leads the programs suggest that sound interesting. Start a file of consumer information and strategies. Think about follow-up action you can take, by yourself or with others.

This is a modest example. Everything mentioned above could take as little as three or four hours before and during the week of the broadcasts themselves. Yet such simple activities could turn what would otherwise be a quickly forgotten TV program into a continuing interest in the broad field of consumer activism. (Or the reverse is possible. The experience might reveal to you that careful consuming is *not* a high priority for you, that you do *not* enjoy the process of learning how to do it, and that you do *not* want to continue down that road. Fine. One of the uses of free learning is to discover what you don't want to learn.)

A third way to build structure into your learning from television is to be *very* selective, searching out programs immediately related to one of your interests or potential interests. In fields like foreign affairs, health, religion, or crime, TV offers a wide range of programs. Moreover, you don't have to confine yourself to what is broadcast. There are libraries of outstanding videotapes. You can view programs at many libraries, or rent or purchase a small video cassette player on which to view leased tapes. (You'll be surprised how inexpensive these have become and how easy they are to use.) Write to the National Association of

Educational Broadcasters, 1346 Connecticut Avenue NW., Washington, D.C. 20036, for sources of information about video cassette rental and purchase.

Several new developments widen the range of television options. One is subscription TV (STV), which frequently offers valuable programs not available on open channels— symphony and ballet performances, Broadway theater, and "live" drama. Another possibility is cable television (CATV), which gives you access to a virtually unlimited number of channels, of which about twenty to forty are currently operational in most systems. Here too the range of programs is broader than on networks and local stations.

If you don't like what is available, there are two other learning options—either become a media activist or make your own programs. Under the Federal Communications Act, television stations must operate in the public interest. They should therefore be responsive to the needs of the public. They want and need to hear from you—your plans and ideas, your efforts to organize to affect local educational offerings. Let the program manager at your local commercial station know that you are interested in what he is doing, that you are aware of how it could add to yours and your family's enjoyment and welfare. Public television stations are even more amenable to viewer suggestions, since their sole purpose is to serve their communities.

A final option, available in a number of cities and spreading rapidly, is to enroll in a "TV College," taking a sequence of credit courses via the tube. The University of Mid-America offers such a program in Kansas, Nebraska, Iowa, and Missouri. Plans to provide such a service in New York and other cities have been proposed. The city colleges of Chicago have been doing it successfully for twenty years.

Vicky Michalik, a mother of two living in a suburb of the city, says Chicago's TV College "saved my brain from rotting. . . . Ever since I got married right after high school, I'd vowed that I'd get my B.A.," she recalls. "Then, just as my first two boys had entered school, and I saw my chance coming, I discovered I was pregnant again. But right after the baby came, someone happened to mention TV college. It was the answer!

"I could get the two boys off to school, and while the baby was napping, I'd take the phone off the hook, pour a second cup of coffee, and turn on the nine o'clock class. If the baby interrupted too many times, I could watch the week's lessons again on the weekend. I took all my basic courses for the degree that way: English, history, other social sciences. The only other way I could have done it would have taken me out of the house four nights a week, which was impossible."

Eight years after starting, Mrs. Michalik got her B.A. in 1974 from Northeastern Illinois College. She got an Associate in Arts degree as a result of TV College. "It's been a long haul," she admits. "I used to think, 'By the time you get the degree, you'll be forty.' But then one day it occurred to me that I was going to be forty anyway, so it was really just a question of whether I wanted to be forty with the degree or without it."

Mrs. Michalik's experience of studying via TV has meant more to her than just the degree. "It's changed my life," she insists. "I was out of touch—whole parts of me were completely unfulfilled. These courses and the people I've met through them have put me in touch with thoughts and feelings of all kinds."

With the momentum provided by the television courses, Mrs. Michalik went back to the classroom. Taking graduate courses even before graduating, she is now looking forward to a career in broadcasting.

Seventy miles from Vicky Michalik's yellow brick house with its well-kept lawn lives another TV College student, Archie Spino. Single and black, he had never aspired to college, nor even finished high school. Archie (which is not his real name) is a prisoner at Joliet State Prison, serving a seven-to-ten-year sentence for stealing cars. In 1973 a counselor at the prison convinced him that he was capable of doing college work. Archie was offered relief from other duties, removal to special quarters, and was allowed to take up to five courses per term.

"I always felt dumb in school," Archie told me, "so I got out of there as fast as I could manage. But this is different. There's no teacher who gives orders and reminds me of my father. There aren't other students who seem to know so much more than I do. It's all up to me, but I can take as much time as I want. And I find that I *can* get it, and that sometimes I even see things that they tell me no other students have come up with before."

By the time he gets out of Joliet, probably in 1977, Archie should have earned his A.A. degree and be eligible for a respectable job or a scholarship for further college work. "No other way I'd have had this chance," he says. "Without that piece of paper, and the feeling that I can learn what I need to know to make it in the straight world, I wouldn't have lasted two months on the street. This way, thanks to the College, I've got at least a chance."

A final exhortation: join, support, and use your local public television station. Public television can be the single most important resource at the free learner's disposal. The enterprise deserves our wholehearted support.

EXPLORING ALTERNATIVES: FROM CHURCHES TO GROWTH CENTERS

Besides the library, you can find in a number of your community's familiar institutions valuable resources for learning that may not have occurred to you.

The Church or Temple*

In most communities across the country the free learner can tap into a never-ending succession of church or temple-sponsored free (or very inexpensive) learning opportunities

---

* This section is the work of Betsy Caprio, a leading exponent of spiritual learning.

—lectures, movies, plays, concerts, and recitals. Some churches and temples, especially in large metropolitan centers, continually run theater, music, and other programs in which both amateurs and professionals take part. The local paper and/or public events broadcasts of radio or TV stations frequently carry notices of these activities. Churches and temples also often offer courses in both religious and secular subjects, although these may not be so widely publicized. Their calendars and bulletin boards, and word-of-mouth, are probably the best sources for such information. A religious education class with a good Biblical scholar can provide some of the best free instruction around, in history as well as religion.

A person specifically interested in religion can easily undertake comparative studies. By visiting a cross-section of the religious institutions in your community, with eyes and ears open and pencil or tape recorder ready, you can design for yourself various courses of study—comparative worship, religious doctrine, religious architecture—and supplement your field work with research at the library and conversations with clergy and informed laymen.

For the church or temple member there are rich learning opportunities beyond those available to the floating free learner. In addition to religious education and scheduled lectures, plays, concerts, and courses, most congregations offer:

- Membership in small groups, either discussion/study groups or interpersonal relations/self-discovery/spiritual growth groups.
- Firsthand experience of the varieties, intricacies, and frustrations of fund raising. Anyone who hangs around a religious institution long enough becomes expert at bazaar running, tag sales, professional money-raising appeals, and sales of "the world's finest chocolate bars" or other toothsome specialties.
- Experience in quantity cookery. If you want to learn about cooking and serving large numbers of people (thinking of opening a restaurant?), let it be known that church-supper organizers can call on you.

- And finally, a very subtle opportunity for field work in humanistic psychology is available to the discerning free learner who is an active church member. In every church or temple there are a few people who are special. The devout might call them holy; psychologists might say they are self-actualized. Whatever the label, getting to know such people is a unique sort of learning. They often become models, or at least touchstones, by which to measure one's own growth.

Settlement Houses, Senior Centers

Settlement houses have for generations provided educational services to the disadvantaged—language training for newly arrived immigrants, consumer education and advocacy training for the poor. Some of the best programs in the arts—performing and visual—have originated in centers like Greenwich House and the Henry Street Settlement in New York, Karamu House in Cleveland, and Hull House in Chicago, to name an outstanding handful.

Another kind of social meeting place, also education-oriented, is the senior center. Older people, an increasing percentage of the total population, are finding new friends and new interests in "Golden Age Club" activities. In addition to recreational games, films, and other entertainment, most senior centers offer classes and work groups, particularly in arts and crafts, and welcome people willing to share their knowledge and skill as instructors.

Education in the Arts

The arts organizations in your community are another set of resources that most people never tap. Community arts centers have burgeoned throughout the country, offering work in theater, dance, film, photography, music, painting, sculpture, and many crafts. To find out what is available near you, talk to your local arts council. Many councils publish a directory of arts resources; they all have listings available in their offices. If there is no local organization, each state has an arts council ready to give you pointers.

In all the arts, you can find practicing artists who also teach. In the plastic arts, you may even want to apprentice yourself to one. In the performing arts, you can work with community theater groups or offer your services as a volunteer to a dance company where you can study techniques and learn informally from the dancers. In music you can usually study with an artist of your choice or join an amateur orchestra or choral society. If none exists, start one.

Most museums have strong educational departments that offer seminars, lectures, study tours, and art courses. Frequently they schedule poetry readings and concerts, free and open to the public. A nominal annual membership fee places you on the mailing list for the monthly calendar that lists rich learning opportunities. Museums are always hungry for volunteers, many of whom are trained as docents who explain the collection to visitors.

"Art is a messy non-academic thing. One learns about art in other than the usual structured approach." This comment was made by a painter friend. One summer while doing graduate work in chemistry in Louisiana in the 1950s, he took a course with a visiting New York artist that changed the direction of his life. He followed the teacher back to New York and set about his own artistic education. My friend, who knew which artists he wanted to study with, learned from Stuart Davis at the New School for Social Research and Ralston Crawford at the Brooklyn Museum. He talked with artists whenever and wherever he could—in class, in bars, in an artists' coffeehouse where he waited on tables to support himself. His self-education included poetry readings at the YMHA and dance classes with Erick Hawkins. In those days sketch sessions at the Art Students League cost only fifty cents and you could draw or paint on your own from a model for several hours. He went to the museums to draw and study the collections.

He also visited art galleries. These he considers the most valuable source of information for the artist because the work is current. Only there and in the artists' studios can you see what is happening today. "By the time works get to the museums," he says, "they are old hat."

And he painted—during every free moment.

On the basis of seven years of free learning, he was accepted in the graduate program of the Newcomb Art School at Tulane University in New Orleans—without ever having had a formal course except that first summer. During graduate school he supported himself and his art with a teaching assistantship. "Art is a personal journey," he concludes. "One should pick and choose artists to study with, and work on your own drawing or paintings for yourself—which is what art is all about."

Learning through Volunteering

A wide range of free learning opportunities opens up in volunteer work with a great diversity of institutions and agencies. A free learner who is willing to volunteer time can get valuable training from hard-working professionals in hospitals and nursing homes; at child care centers and in programs for the elderly; at museums, arts centers, schools; and in many other kinds of recreational, educational, and correctional programs. It's easy. Make an appointment with the administrator or director of volunteers of a program in which you would like some experience. Tell that person what you'd like to do, what you have to offer, why you are volunteering. (Be brief—these are busy people.) If your offer is accepted, be reliable. If you are alert to the functioning of the program, you will gain knowledge and skills, become familiar with the problems of the work, be able to test your interest in the field, and perhaps garner some good references for your portfolio.

Several national clearinghouses will provide leads to local

organizations and other information about the how and why of volunteer work.

- The Commission on Voluntary Service and Action, 475 Riverside Drive, New York, New York 10027.
- The National Center for Voluntary Action, 1785 Massachusetts Avenue, NW., Washington, D.C. 20036,
- The Center for a Voluntary Society, 1705 LaSalle, NW., Washington, D.C. 20005.

Apprenticeships and Other Training Opportunities

In learning by doing, the steps beyond volunteer work are the various internships, apprenticeships, the so-called "field experiences" provided as part of college programs, as well as subsistence jobs in public interest organizations. Unlike volunteer work, these are usually full time and sometimes carry a nominal salary. They are worth considering for a working vacation; or, if you are unemployed anyhow and want to take advantage of the situation, they will give you exposure to a new field. Check with your state employment agency, which can provide the address of your state's Apprenticeship Information Center, and write for the booklet *The National Apprenticeship Program,* available from the Bureau of Apprenticeship and Training, Manpower Administration, U.S. Department of Labor, Washington, D.C. 20212.

For less conventional fields try Pacific High School's Apprenticeship Service Program, 12100 Skyline Boulevard, Los Gatos, California 95030. "We want to help provide contact between apprentice and master, person and mentor, learner and teacher all over the country. When someone tells us what he/she would like to do, we will let them know if we know of any people who would/could help and/or try to find people," the Program says.

Some apprenticeships cost money. In the arts, for example, an apprentice may pay a monthly fee for the privilege of working with an established artist.

Still another source of "non-traditional education" are the thousands of training programs offered by national associations of all kinds. Very often these provide first-rate instruction more relevant to the mature person's needs than the more "ivory tower" instruction provided by liberal arts colleges. Here are a few of the most active: the American Association of Retired Persons, the National Retired Teachers Association, the Association of Junior Leagues, the League of Women Voters and other women's clubs, B'nai B'rith, Hadassah, the National Conference of Christians and Jews, the Young Men's and Young Women's Christian and Hebrew Associations, the U.S. Committee for UNICEF, the Red Cross, the AFL-CIO and other labor groups, the Chamber of Commerce, the Foreign Policy Association, and major fraternal and religious organizations.

National associations that offer such education are members of the Council of National Organizations for Adult Education, 819 18th Street NW., Washington, D.C. 20006, which can give you useful information. And don't forget that it may be possible, if you're interested, to get credit for the courses you take from the Office on Non-Collegiate Sponsored Instruction (see page 161).

"Inner Learning"—Therapists, Gurus, Growth Groups

This book has stressed that the basis of free learning is your awareness of your own interests, needs, and goals. But getting to "Know Thyself" is a process in which many of us can use help. Today such help is at hand in almost embarrassing and confusing abundance. Americans have turned to, and invented, a remarkable range of mental-health and mind-expanding techniques over the past decade. "More than 130 different approaches are now being purveyed in the marketplace of psychosocial therapies," observes Morris Parloff, who monitors them from the National Institute of Mental Health. "New schools emerge constantly, heralded by claims that they provide better treatment, amelioration, or management of the problems and neuroses of the day."

To the major schools of therapy—classical psychoanalysis and its derivatives, behavior therapies that follow B. F. Skinner's methods of "conditioning," humanistic therapies that stress self-actualization, and transpersonal therapies that strive for cosmic consciousness—have been added such *sui generis* school a primal therapy, transactional analysis (Eric Berne's "I'm O.K., You're O.K." system), family therapy, and socially radical therapies (such as feminist therapy) which insist that the patient's problems stem in large part from the structure of society, which therefore must be reformed.

From the point of view of the individual free learner, this proliferation of approaches means that in most communities some choice among competing schools is readily available. For example, in most cities of reasonable size you can now find a variety of growth groups available: encounter, sensitivity, etc. Someone is likely to be offering each of the major kinds of mental or spiritual training at moderate cost: assertiveness, transcendental meditation, transactional analysis. There is probably a growth center of some kind within a hundred miles, at which more specialized or intensive experiences are available: residential weekends, longer courses. And, of course, professional practitioners of the major therapies can usually be found for individual treatment.

No one really knows how to choose between these various forms of "inner learning." Dr. Parloff offers as "consumer guidance" the following findings that emerge from the studies that have been conducted of the major therapies' results:

Most forms of psychotherapy are effective with about two-thirds of their non-psychotic patients. Treated patients show significantly more improvement in thought, mood, personality, and behavior than do comparable samples of untreated patients.

... Apparent differences in the relative effectiveness of different psychotherapies gradually disappear with time. Although most studies report that similar proportions of patients benefit from all tested forms of therapy, the possibility remains open that different therapies may effect different kinds of change. All forms of psychotherapy tend to be reasonably useful for patients who are highly motivated, experience acute discomfort, show a high degree of personality organization, are reasonably well educated, have had some history of social success and recognition, are reflective, and can experience and express emotion.

Since this profile fits the free learner, it suggests that the right approach to making one's way through the teeming bazaar of therapies and self-actualization techniques is to look on the process of choosing as itself a learning project. And here too the inquiry begins with oneself. The more you know about your own needs and style, the more sensibly you will select your experiences or treatment. "When the patient is 'therapist-shopping,'" concludes Dr. Parloff, "it is wise for him to select carefully from among an array of qualified therapists the one whose style of relating is acceptable to him—and preferably from a school whose philosophy, values, and goals are most congenial to his own." (There are a number of books that are helpful here, such as *The New Psychotherapies*, Robert A. Harper, Spectrum Books [Prentice-Hall], 1975; and *When to See a Psychologist*, Dr. Lee M. Shulman and Joan Kennedy Taylor [Award Books], 1969.)

DO-IT-YOURSELF COLLEGES

Another grass-roots movement serving free learners is what I call the "do-it-yourself colleges." These enterprises differ from learning exchanges and small special interest groups because an array of organized courses is offered. But do-it-yourself college courses differ from those at the established adult schools too, in that they are a lot cheaper, more convenient, more accessible, more varied, more interesting, and in many cases more rewarding.

The most widespread type of do-it-yourself college is the free university. There are about two hundred of these around the country at present, according to the Free U Network (FUN), which serves as a clearinghouse for the movement. Many began on or near campuses in the 1960s, offering counterculture and radical courses to complement the conventional courses available from the college faculty. Students and young faculty members taught one another. "Everyone can learn, everyone can teach" became the motto. Courses were offered free or at low cost, in borrowed facilities, people's apartments, or parks.

In recent years many free universities have shifted toward a more balanced curriculum, and new ones have started which are designed to serve adults in a wide range of ways. Some put out catalogs with up to two hundred courses; some even have permanent facilities of their own. Certificates are available for completion of courses in some FU's, and one charges twenty-five cents for a "diploma."

At the University of Man in Manhattan, Kansas, a recent catalog listed courses in traffic laws, improvement of nursing homes, batik, pottery, edible plants, water color painting, homemade root beer, stress management, Yoga after forty, Pierre Teilhard de Chardin, science/sex/society, Socrates/Buddha/Confucius, rationale for liberal thought, how to love your body, preparing 1976 taxes, and bartending. The entire catalog was thirty-two pages long, even though it was a summer edition, and in the front it asked people to volunteer to teach new courses the following autumn in basic plumbing, folk guitar, natural eye improvement, bookkeeping, mime, languages, interior decorating, martial arts, assertiveness, and many other subjects.

Courses are offered at UFM House, the university's headquarters, as well as in borrowed space on the Kansas State University campus, in the Manhattan Public Library, and in instructors' homes. Some meet only once (pressed flower arrangements), some for three or four sessions, some longer; some are open-ended, depending on the wishes of the group that comes together. All courses are free. (Some FUs do charge.)

UFM is supported by the Kansas State University Division of Continuing Education, the Student Government Association, the Manhattan Chapter of the United Way, and two federal programs. But free universities can be set up completely independent of campuses.

One example is the Beacon Hill Free School in Boston. "We're beginning our ninth year of free courses this term," says Jack Powers, the school's founder and coordinator. "We've offered over three hundred in all, to thousands of people of all ages, at no cost. Our purpose is simply to get people of all ages together, using the resources of the community, human and material. We continue to thrive because instructors are willing to volunteer their time and services and because neighbors and neighborhood organizations are willing to donate unused space in the evenings. What small costs accrue, for printing, mailing, and the like, are met by donations from kind friends and an occasional benefit."

A typical catalog of the Free School lists a variety of courses: life drawing, bicycle repair, languages including Portuguese and Russian, creative movement, Beethoven, and welfare advocacy training. As to deciding what and how to teach, Powers explains: "The list of offerings is shaped each term at the General Meetings held every three months where anyone is free to offer a course and anyone is free to take what is offered. What administration there is is performed by a few people, in their spare time."

For a directory of free universities throughout the country send one dollar to the Free University Network (FUN), 615 Fairchild Terrace, Manhattan, Kansas 66502. FUN compiled the listing of free universities which appears below, and is itself a remarkable network of free learners.

A do-it-yourself college may develop from a special situation or circumstance. That is the case with a group of 3M Company employees in St. Paul, Minnesota, who formed what is now a thriving "Language Society." It started simply. Several people who knew German began getting together in a cafeteria to maintain their fluency. Others thought the idea sounded interesting and wanted to join in, even though they didn't know German. Still others hoped the program could be broadened to include other languages, as it was.

According to James Hendricks, one of the founders, "it was not easy. It was apparent that we would need a quiet place to meet, teaching materials (textbooks, tapes, or records) for those just beginning, equipment to play the tapes, and a modest investment to get started. We now have some six hundred members per year, more quiet places to meet, and we are just now furnishing a 'Learning Center' for additional study, independent of the teacher."

Initial funding was provided by the employees' club. Membership dues of two dollars a year help defray expenses; teaching materials are available to students at cost. Midday classes are free and take up thirty minutes of the lunch hour. Evening classes are twenty dollars for twenty hours of instruction; fourteen dollars for fourteen hours. There are three sessions per year, each for seven or ten weeks. The core of the program is a volunteer teaching staff —people committed to an idea and an ideal.

Textbooks are used, but as Esther Piper, coordinator of the Language Society, says, "since we manufacture tape recorders, magnetic tape, overhead projectors, and other supporting teaching aids, we make considerable use of them in our classes. For example, many of our students have found that the small cassette tape recorders are very helpful in practicing at home between class lessons. We do assign homework, but we are emphasizing the enjoyment of learning a language rather than the strict pedagogical approach —the emphasis on conversation rather than grammar. The motivation and degree of interest of a student determine his progress."

Festival Evenings, with dinner and the evening devoted to one country, are held periodically to stimulate and maintain interest. The food, music, and entertainment are as authentic as possible.

An important outgrowth of this society is the building of a resource for 3M of employees with capabilities for translating, interpreting, and communication with subsidiary personnel. And for the community as a whole it provides a resource for schools on Career Days, for other companies on ways to start their own programs, and for agencies such as Travelers Aid and various counseling services, offering interpreting on an emergency basis.

The Institute for Retired Professionals, located at the New School for Social Research in New York City, is a program for, of, and created by its six hundred members, rather than something simply made available to them by an institution. For an annual fee of $200, a member has the opportunity to create, conduct, and attend institute learning groups of all kinds, as well as to enroll free in any other course offered in the New School's brimming catalog. A participant could, if he wished, come to school every day—meet with one group in the morning, have lunch in the cafeteria with fellow students, join another group in the afternoon, and stay around one evening a week for a more conventional kind of course taught by a professional teacher. Many do just this, becoming virtual "students in residence."

The institute's member-taught courses, over sixty in all, include languages, a course called "Our Changing Culture," workshops in writing, dramatics, biomedical developments, and Jewish history. Each is coordinated by an institute member who is himself a student, and in each the participants take an active role: presenting papers, conducting discussions, performing, and organizing field trips. Retired doctors, dentists, business executives, bankers, artists, journalists, teachers, attorneys, and engineers are finding second careers as teachers—of one another.

"When I founded the institute in 1962," Hy Hirsch, proprietor of this miniature Platonic academy, explains, "there was no place where creative, educated retirees could continue to grow intellectually. My approach was to challenge them to create their own program, their own place, a little world from which they could reach out to other people and to new ideas."

Clearly the institute is no answer for the mass of retired people in the United States. But it works splendidly for those with a strong cultural background, a good deal of vitality and initiative, and $200. The idea is spreading, with Hirsch's encouragement. The institute has already sparked replications in several other Manhattan neighborhoods (to spare students the hassle of traveling to the New School), as well as self-contained institutes in Boston, Philadelphia, Cleveland, San Francisco, San Diego, and other centers containing a critical mass of intellectually enterprising retirees.

Some Free Universities Around the Country

ALABAMA

Extracurricular Studies Program
Union Building, Room 316
Auburn University
Auburn, Alabama 36830

Free University
University of Alabama
Box 1247, c/o SGA
Huntsville, Alabama 35801

Experimental College
University of South Alabama
Mobile, Alabama 36688

ARIZONA

Tucson Free University
715 N. Park
Tucson, Arizona 85719

ARKANSAS

Free University
c/o United Campus Ministry
902 W. Maple
Fayetteville, Arkansas 72701

Open University
University of Arkansas at Little
    Rock
35th and University
c/o Community Affairs
    Committee
Little Rock, Arkansas 72204

New Schools Exchange
Pettigrew, Arkansas 72752

The Community Center of
    Learning
311 W. B Street
Russellville, Arkansas 72801

CALIFORNIA

Humboldt Free University
P.O. Box 1023
Arcata, California 95221

Microcosm Free University
1417 Grant Street
Berkeley, California 94703

Jackson Valley Community Center
c/o Gayle Murrey
Branscomb, California 95417

Andorra II
27 Wilson Street
Daly City, California 94014

Experimental College
University of California, Davis
Davis, California 95616

Experimental College
Fresno City College
Fresno, California 93704

Experimental College
California State University
Letters and Science, Room 78
Fullerton, California 92631

Integrative Learning System
326 W. Chevy Chase Drive 11
Glendale, California 91204

Experimental College
c/o ASICI
University of California, Irvine
Irvine, California 92647

Communiversity West
Associated Students
California State University
6101 E. 7th
Long Beach, California 90801

Experimental College
Student Activities Office
Administration 123
California State University
Los Angeles, California 90037

Experimental College
c/o Associated Students
University of Southern California
Student Union 321
Los Angeles, California 90024

UCLA Experimental College
310 Kerckhoff Hall
308 Westwood Plaza
Los Angeles, California 90024

University for Man
Monterey Peninsula College
980 Fremont, Room E4
Monterey, California 93940

Experimental College
California State University
18111 Nordhoff Street
Northridge, California 91330

Open Education Exchange
6526 Telegraph Avenue
Oakland, California 94609

Alternative Education
ASSC
California State University
Sacramento, California 95819

Shasta School
101 Ross Avenue
San Anselmo, California 94960

Experimental College
Aztec Center, Lower 178
California State University
San Diego, California 92115

Ocean Beach Community School
4854 Lotus Street
San Diego, California 92107

Communiversity
451 Judah Street
San Francisco, California 94122

Experimental College
ASSJSC
College Union Bldg.
South 9th Street
San Jose, California 95114

Experimental College
City College at San Francisco
50 Phelan Avenue
San Francisco, California 94112

Freedom School
245 Mississippi Street
San Francisco, California 94107

Heliotrope
21 Columbus
San Francisco, California 94111

Lavendar U
121 Leavenworth
San Francisco, California 94102

Liberation School
2323 Market Street
San Francisco, California 94114

Orpheus
1119 Geary Boulevard
San Francisco, California 94109

Outlaw Institute
238 San Jose Avenue
San Francisco, California 94112

Experimental College
Associated Student Union
312-A University of Southern
California
University Park, California 90007

Free University
10126 Storr Road
Windsor, California 95492

COLORADO

Community Free School
885 Arapahoe
Boulder, Colorado 80302

Denver Free University
Box 18455, 1122 E. 17th Avenue
Denver, Colorado 80218

Free University
Route 1, Box 113
Durango, Colorado 81301

University II
c/o Student Center
Colorado State University
Fort Collins, Colorado 80521

Snow Mountain Free U
Box 558
Granby, Colorado 80446

Lambor Valley School
Route 1
Hotchkiss, Colorado 81419

Free University
Route 1, Box 544
La Jara, Colorado 81140

Yampa Open University
Good News Building
Steamboat Springs, Colorado
80477

CONNECTICUT

Free School
Box 404-A, Yale Station
New Haven, Connecticut 06520

Experimental College, U-8
University of Connecticut
Storrs, Connecticut 06268

DELAWARE

Delaware Free University
104 Pencader Dining Hall
   Building
University of Delaware
Newark, Delaware 19711

DISTRICT OF COLUMBIA

New University
Suite 605
1718 P Street NW.
Washington, D.C. 20036

Open University of Washington
3100 Connecticut Avenue NW.,
   Suite 300
Washington, D.C. 20008

Washington Area Free U
1724 20th Street NW.
Washington, D.C. 20009

FLORIDA

Chai Community
Temple Israel of Miami
137 NE. 19th Street
Miami, Florida 33132

F.I.A. International University
c/o SGA, Attn. Glenn Jones
Tamiami Trail
Miami, Florida 33132

Center for Participant Education
251 University Union
Florida State University
Tallahassee, Florida 32306

The Common Learning Network
c/o Student Government, UC
   156E
University of South Florida
Tampa, Florida 33620

GEORGIA

Free University
Student Center
Georgia Institute of Technology
Atlanta, Georgia 30332

ILLINOIS

Free School, SGA Council
Student Center, Third Floor
Southern Illinois University
Carbondale, Illinois 62901

Common Ground
809 S. 5th
Champaign, Illinois 61820

Southwestern Illinois Learning
   Co-op
Box 67, Student Activities Office
Southern Illinois University
Edwardsville, Illinois 62025

Free University
Knox College
Galesburg, Illinois 61401

Communiversity
Office of Academic Services
Western Illinois University
Macomb, Illinois 61455

INDIANA

Free University
Union Board Office
Indiana Memorial Union
Bloomington, Indiana 47401

FLEX Free University
c/o Bethlehem Lutheran Church
526 E. 52nd Street
Indianapolis, Indiana 46205

Free University
Student Government Association
Indiana Central College
1400 W. Hanna
Indianapolis, Indiana 46206

Free University of Muncie
Student Center B-3
Ball State University
Muncie, Indiana 47306

IOWA

Ames Free University
Iowa State University
Ames, Iowa 50010

New College
Drake University
29th Street and University Avenue
Des Moines, Iowa 50311

Action Studies Program
300 Jefferson Building
Iowa City, Iowa 52242

KANSAS

Community Education Project
Abilene Public Library
Abilene, Kansas 67410

Clay County Community
  Education
Episcopal Church
6th and Clark
Clay Center, Kansas 67432

Neosho River Free School
Union Activity Council
Emporia Kansas State College
Emporia, Kansas 66801

Hoxie Community Education
  Project
Northwest Kansas Library System
Hoxie, Kansas 67740

Kansas University Free University
Kansas Union, SUA Office
University of Kansas
Lawrence, Kansas 66045

St. Mary College Free University
c/o Sister Mary Beth Kelly
St. Mary College
Leavenworth, Kansas 66048

The Other Term
c/o Fred Ray
Bethany College
Lindsborg, Kansas 67056

University for Man
615 Fairchild Terrace
Manhattan, Kansas 66502

Marshall County Community
  Education
P.O. Box 365
Marysville, Kansas 66508

Norton Community Education
  Project
Public Library
Norton, Kansas 67654

Oberlin Community Education
 Project
Public Library
Oberlin, Kansas 67749

Little House
901 N. 9th Street
Salina, Kansas 67401

Washburn Free University
Washburn University
Topeka, Kansas 66621

Wichita Free University
Interchange
Box 56, Wichita State University
Wichita, Kansas 67208

KENTUCKY

Free University
Student Center, Room 204
University of Kentucky
Lexington, Kentucky 40506

Free University
SGA Office, Student Center
University of Louisville
Louisville, Kentucky 40208

Free University of Murray
Box 3094, University Station
Murray, Kentucky 42071

University for Free Men
Student Association Office
Eastern Kentucky University
Richmond, Kentucky 40475

LOUISIANA

LSU Union Informal Classes
Attention: Shirley Plakidas
P.O. Box BU, University Station
Baton Rouge, Louisiana 70893

Union Craft Shop Courses
Box 2611
University of Southwestern
 Louisiana
Lafayette, Louisiana 70501

Free University of New Orleans
New Orleans Public Library
219 Loyola Avenue
New Orleans, Louisiana 70140

MAINE

Abenaki Experimental College
Memorial Union
University of Maine
Orono, Maine 04473

The Other Program
University of Maine at Portland
96 Falmouth Street
Portland, Maine 04103

Experimental College
Colby College
Waterville, Maine 04901

MARYLAND

Aquarian University
811 N. Charles Street
Baltimore, Maryland 21201

Baltimore Free University
Office of the Chaplain
Johns Hopkins University
Baltimore, Maryland 21218

The Baltimore School
P.O. Box 4833
Baltimore, Maryland 21211

Opening Networks
613 Winan Way
Baltimore, Maryland 21229

Maryland Free University
Student Government Association
University of Maryland
College Park, Maryland 20742

MASSACHUSETTS

Beacon Hill Free School
315 Cambridge Street
Boston, Massachusetts 02114

Boston Community School
107 South Street
Boston, Massachusetts 02130

The Free School
c/o George Sherman Union
    Building
Room 435
Boston University
Boston, Massachusetts 02215

Free University of the Fenway
68 St. Stephen Street
Boston, Massachusetts 02115

The Hillel House
University within a University
233 Bay State Road
Boston, Massachusetts 02115

Smith Experimental College
150 Elm Street
Northampton, Massachusetts
    01060

Miniversity
c/o Your Place
806 Main Street
Worcester, Massachusetts 01610

MICHIGAN

Thomas Jefferson College
Grand Valley State College
Allendale, Michigan 49426

Free University of Ann Arbor
c/o UAC, Michigan Union
Ann Arbor, Michigan 48104

Free Community School
Project Headline
13627 Gratiot
Detroit, Michigan 48205

Free University
University Student Government
University of Detroit
4001 W. McNichols
Detroit, Michigan 48221

Wayne State Free University
343 University Center
Detroit, Michigan

University for Man
Michigan State University
325 Student Services Building
East Lansing, Michigan 48823

Free University
Kalamazoo College
Kalamazoo, Michigan 49001

MINNESOTA

Judson Life School
4101 Harriet Avenue S.
Minneapolis, Minnesota 55409

Minnesota Free University
c/o James Park
1417 First Avenue S. #210
Minneapolis, Minnesota 55403

Free University
St. Olaf College
Northfield, Minnesota 55057

MISSISSIPPI

Free University
c/o YMCA
Mississippi State University
State College, Mississippi 39762

MISSOURI

Communiversity
c/o Student Government
University of Missouri
Columbia, Missouri 65201

Communiversity
5100 Rockhill Road
University of Missouri at Kansas
    City
Kansas City, Missouri 64110

Free University
University Union Program Office
Central Missouri State University
Warrensburg, Missouri 64093

MONTANA

Community University
SUB, Room 202
Montana State University
Bozeman, Montana 59715

Free University
Student Center
University of Montana
Missoula, Montana 59801

NEBRASKA

Nebraska Free University
Room 334, Nebraska Union
University of Nebraska
Lincoln, Nebraska 68508

Free University
University of Nebraska
c/o Academic Resource Center
Box 688, Downtown Station
Omaha, Nebraska 68101

NEW HAMPSHIRE

Everybody's School
c/o Center for Human Survival
52 Main Street, Westboro
West Lebanon, New Hampshire
    03784

NEW MEXICO

The Glorieta School
Route 1, Box 5A
Glorieta, New Mexico 87535

Lama Foundation
Box 449
San Cristobal, New Mexico 87564

Santa Fe Free School
Canyon Road
Sante Fe, New Mexico 87501

Taos Community University
General Delivery
Taos, New Mexico 87571

NEW JERSEY

The Community House
Seton Hall
South Orange, New Jersey 07079

Free University
Newark State College
Union, New Jersey 07083

NEW YORK

Albany Free School
20 Oxford Road
Albany, New York 12203

Clinton Free School
P.O. Box 73
Clinton, New York 13323

Storefront
140 W. State Street
Ithaca, New York 14850

Apple Skills Exchange
Jack Johnson
137 Fifth Avenue
New York, New York 10010

Emmaus
241 E. 116th Street
New York, New York 10029

Experimental College
343 Finley Student Center, CCNY
133rd Street at Convent Avenue
New York, New York 10031

FreeSpace
c/o Appleseed
339 Lafayette Place
New York, New York 10012

Open Space
Loeb Student Center 109
566 La Guardia Place
New York, New York 10012

Real University of the Streets
130 E. 7th Street
New York, New York 10009

Communiversity
c/o VSC
713 Monroe
Rochester, New York 14666

Free University
Rochester Institute of Technology
1 Lomb Memorial Drive
Rochester, New York 14623

Free University
Le Moyne College
Syracuse, New York 13214

OHIO

Free University
John Carroll University
Cleveland, Ohio 44118

Columbus Free University
Plantland, c/o Wesley Found
82 E. 16th Avenue
Columbus, Ohio 43015

Ohio Wesleyan Free University
Ohio Wesleyan University
Delaware, Ohio 43015

OKLAHOMA

The Extra-Curriculum
Center for Student Development
University of Oklahoma
Norman, Oklahoma 73069

Free University
Oral Roberts University
777 S. Lewis
Tulsa, Oklahoma 74105

Praxis Project
Canterbury Center
2839 E. 5th
Tulsa, Oklahoma 74104

OREGON

ASOSU Experimental College
Associated Students
Memorial Union, Oregon State
  University
Corvallis, Oregon 97331

Blake College
300½ N. Jefferson
Eugene, Oregon 97402

Search
ERB Memorial Union
University of Oregon
Eugene, Oregon 97401

Lewis and Clark Experimental
  College
Box 301
Portland, Oregon 97403

PENNSYLVANIA

Free University
Edinboro State College
P.O. Box 319
Edinboro, Pennsylvania 16412

College Union
LaSalle College
Philadelphia, Pennsylvania 19141

Free University
Box 95, SAC
Temple University
13th and Montgomery
Philadelphia, Pennsylvania 19122

Free University
c/o Associated Students
St. Joseph's College
Philadelphia, Pennsylvania 19131

Free University of Pennsylvania
COS Office, Houston Hall
3417 Spruce St.
Philadelphia, Pennsylvania 19104

Jewish Free University
Psychology Department
University of Pennsylvania
Philadelphia, Pennsylvania 19104

Neighborhood Talent Registry
612 Dallas Avenue
Pittsburgh, Pennsylvania 15217

Penn State Free University
233 HUB, Penn Student Union
University Park, Pennsylvania
  16802

Villanova Free University
c/o The Villanovan
Villanova University
Villanova, Pennsylvania 19085

SOUTH CAROLINA

Free University, Russell House
Box 85141, University Union
University of South Carolina
Columbia, South Carolina 29208

SOUTH DAKOTA

Free University
UMHE
South Dakota State University
802 11th Avenue
Brookings, South Dakota 57006

Free University
Dakota State College
103 N. Liberty
Madison, South Dakota 57402

TENNESSEE

College of Man
University of Tennessee
Chattanooga, Tennesse 37401

Free University
Student Senate Office
University of Tennessee
Knoxville, Tennessee 37916

Free University of Nashville
Box 3975, Station B
Vanderbilt University
Nashville, Tennessee 37235

TEXAS

Texas Union Informal Classes
University of Texas
Austin, Texas 78712

Free University Committee
Texas A & M University
P.O. Box 5718, Memorial Student
 Center
College Station, Texas 77844

The Short Course
Mountain View College
4849 W. Illinois
Dallas, Texas 75211

Southern Methodist University
Room 209, Student Center
Student Activities Directorate
Dallas, Texas 75275

Free University of Denton
Box 13766, NTSU Station
Denton, Texas 76203

Terry Marlow
Free University
3917 W. 7th Street (garage)
Fort Worth, Texas 76107

Sundry School
Campus Activities Department
University of Houston
Houston, Texas 77004

Free University
University Center Programs
Texas Tech University
P.O. Box 4310
Lubbock, Texas 79409

Creative Curriculum College
Eastfield College
3737 Motley
Mesquite, Texas 75149

Free U Committee
University Center, Box 3056
Stephen Austin State University
Nacogdoches, Texas 75961

Experimental College
Trinity University
715 Stadium Drive
San Antonio, Texas 78284

San Antonio Free University
1136 W. Woodlawn
San Antonio, Texas 78201

Free University
Student Government
Baylor University
Waco, Texas 76703

The Open School
P.O. Box 352
McQueeney, Texas 78123

ASUSU PREP, UMC 01
Utah State University
Logan, Utah 84322

Free University of Utah
Student Activities Center
University of Utah
Salt Lake City, Utah 84112

Experimental College
203 HUB
University of Washington
Seattle, Washington 98195

Free University
Cartwright Center
University of Wisconsin
LaCrosse, Wisconsin 54601

Whole Earth Learning
  Community
817 E. Johnson Street
Madison, Wisconsin 53703

Milwaukee Free University
1336 N. Astor
Milwaukee, Wisconsin 53202

Marquette Free University
ASMU
600 N. 14th Street
Milwaukee, Wisconsin 53233

Multiversity
Box 3625, University Station
Laramie, Wyoming 80271

MAKING THE CAMPUS CONNECTION

Whether or not you are seeking credit toward a degree, you should investigate the opportunities for free learning at your local college or university. There are ways to use these institutions that go far beyond merely matriculating.

Many colleges have thriving Schools of Continuing Education which offer marvelous courses on a wide range of subjects. Often the faculty is drawn from the ranks of highly successful business, community, and intellectual leaders who serve as "adjunct faculty" and make fascinating teachers. The charges are much less than for credit courses, and you can create your own curriculum. These courses are the free learner's best academic buy.

The campus is a gathering place of co-learners; potential teachers are not limited to just the professors. Hundreds of activities—ranging from interest groups to government-funded projects—never appear in the catalog. Some of these opportunities may be more useful to you than course work, and they are often cheaper and more flexible.

As a starter, attend some special events on campus. All colleges run programs of lectures, concerts, movies, plays, conferences, and exhibits. Find out from the campus public relations office how you can get a list of these events. If they don't publish a calendar, encourage them to do so and to set up a mailing list of interested townspeople.

You may also be able to use the library. At some colleges library privileges are available for a modest fee. At many public colleges around the country, the college library is completely accessible to all the people of the community.

A campus is a fine place to start a learning exchange, plug into a network, or make your own matches and contacts with fellow learners. Put notices on the bulletin boards and in the school paper. Find out what campus organizations deal with matters you're interested in or could be interested in.

Figure what *you* would like to get from the college and ask for it. This method is increasingly effective because most colleges need and want to serve their communities better. At a typical community college, for example, a group of older people turned up one evening for a meeting of the administration and demanded a program geared to their needs. Their representatives were appointed to a planning committee and came up with a program dealing with consumer affairs, sex after sixty, and great books. At least two institutions will provide a teacher for any fifteen people who get together to learn, and find them a place to meet in their own neighborhood: the Vermont Community Colleges and the Institute for Study by Older Adults in Brooklyn, New York.

Another attractive new option is the "educational vacation"—also known as the "weekend college," "institute," "suitcase seminar," or just plain "conference." These brief residential programs can be exciting, intense, and refreshing experiences, particularly if you want to poke a toe into the academic waters before you dive back in. They may be located on campuses, or if you prefer you can find them in a wide variety of other environments: rural and wilderness areas, at retreats run by religious organizations, at conference centers sponsored by business and professional groups, and even at sea! *The Weekend Education Source Book* by Wilbur Cross (Harper's Magazine Press) is a paperback guide and catalog listing 320 programs throughout the country.

TUTOR IN YOUR MAILBOX

Another opportunity for free learners offered by many universities and by private training schools is correspondence study. It has some very pronounced advantages, the obvious one being its flexibility: you can work whenever you like, in whatever manner you like. You can do two lessons a week or one a month, though most counselors urge that you move through the course briskly to maintain your interest. The cost is modest. Universities charge about fifteen dollars per credit hour, which means that an entire course, including books, can cost less than sixty dollars.

Knowing in advance what correspondence study is like can help you decide whether it's for you. You'll start with a booklet of twenty or twenty-five lessons and assignments plus a textbook you can either buy locally or order from the school. Each lesson usually includes some assigned reading in the text and/or notes in the syllabus. There is also a short test or essay keyed to each of the readings, which when completed is sent to the instructor. Within a week to ten days the submission comes back marked with marginal notations and perhaps a note from the instructor.

Before the last lesson, you arrange to take an examination, which is sent to some local school person, clergyman, or librarian. Some schools are experimenting with more feedback options: the chance to phone the instructor now and then, the use of such audiovisual materials as cassettes, and even videotapes as part of the package.

Colleges and universities around the country—including the Universities of California, Chicago, Kansas, Nebraska, Oklahoma, and Wisconsin, Indiana University, and Pennsylvania State University—offer 500-odd correspondence courses. In addition the Independent Study Program of the New York State Education Department offers more than eighty-five undergraduate study courses in thirty fields. Many are supplemented with films, videotapes, cassettes, slides, and laboratory kits. All programs can be applied toward an Empire State College degree. (See section on New Routes to Your Diploma, page 151.)

The nation's first B.A. by correspondence is currently being designed. The Committee on Institutional Cooperation, the academic consortium of the Big Ten Universities and the University of Chicago, has announced plans for a series of new correspondence courses which—along with home study courses now in use—will provide all the credits needed for the bachelor's degree.

With the support of a $486,000 Carnegie Corporation grant, the six CIC universities engaged in correspondence education —Illinois, Indiana, Iowa, Michigan, Minnesota, and Wisconsin—will jointly prepare some twenty-four new upper division courses over the next four years designed to round out full majors in English literature, history, business, education, economics, and sociology. Credits earned by correspondence will be accepted in new external degree programs—courses of study which require no campus residence—at Indiana University and the University of Wisconsin and in the proposed Bachelor of Liberal Studies program to be offered by Iowa's three regental universities (Iowa, Iowa State, and Northern Iowa). In addition, CIC correspondence credit will be fully accepted for the Regents' External Degree Program of the University of the State of New York, and some CIC students will receive their bachelor's degrees from Albany.

Information on Correspondence Study

For a booklet containing further information for prospective students, *Tips on Home Study Schools:*
Council of Better Business Bureaus, Inc.
1150 17th Street NW.
Washington, D.C. 20036
For a catalog of college and university correspondence courses and a booklet on home study:
National University Extension Association
1 Dupont Circle
Washington, D.C. 20036
For a list of accredited private correspondence schools:
National Home Study Council
1601 18th Street NW.
Washington, D.C. 20009
Another good source:
Independent Study Program
State Education Department
99 Washington Avenue
Albany, New York 12210

Inquiries should be directed to Frederick H. Jackson, Director, Committee on Institutional Cooperation, Suite 130, 820 Davis Street, Evanston, Illinois 60201.

There are also accredited private correspondence schools like International Correspondence Schools (ICS), LaSalle, and Advanced Schools. Their courses are generally even better designed and more pleasant to use than those produced by universities. These institutions can put more money into the development of their courses than the universities can, so they usually include kits, multimedia, and other learning aids in their lessons. Of course they are also much more expensive.

I've taken two correspondence courses myself. In one on the poetry of Yeats, my teacher, who was a quite distinguished scholar in the field, marked my essays himself. When I took the other course, in general semantics, I combined it with a series of filmed lectures by S. I. Hayakawa borrowed from the library. Both of these courses were better than most of the courses I had in college, and have stayed with me longer. In both cases I felt in touch with a vibrant teacher—in the first through correspondence with a real authority, in the second mainly through the Hayakawa films, since the assignments in the semantics course were graded by a nondescript who either gave very little himself or had very little to give. The experience illustrates the need for initiative in this kind of study. If I had not used the Hayakawa films to liven things up and enrich the course, it probably would have been a failure.

THE CASSETTE CURRICULUM

Let us now praise the versatile, economical, easy-to-use tape cassette, which almost overnight has become an indispensable and ubiquitous tool for learning. Most libraries have a whole bookcase of cassettes to lend. There are superb catalogs (see list on page 148) that give you access to tapes by experts on practically any subject.

The biggest catalog, which you will certainly want to obtain (it is free), comes from the Center for Cassette Studies. The two-volume set lists thousands of tapes, arranged in twenty-three subject areas, under such headings as authors, composers, statesmen, journalism, literature, science, religion, and the arts. Each cassette is packaged with a listing of suggested readings and a study guide.

The other tape catalogs listed here have one or another special slant. The Living Library, for example, specializes in social change in education, ecology, and politics. The Tape Rental Library, on the other hand, specializes in offerings for business. For ninety-five dollars a year you can borrow two at a time. Included are management seminars, sales courses, and discussions on advertising, real estate, insurance, and so on. The University of California Extension Division began in 1975 to offer a series of courses for credit on cassettes, which are available through libraries.

You will undoubtedly come upon tape services in your own major fields of interest. For example, the Behavioral Science Tape Rental Service offers a subscription service that gives you borrowing access to its library of over five hundred tapes for a single annual membership. You get a selection of six cassettes at a time, of your choice; the topics range from "Marital and Sexual Counseling" to "Special Clinical Problems in Intensive Psychotherapy" to "Multimodel Behavior Therapy." For the aspiring professional this specialized material can provide convenient access to a wealth of new material.

The professional association in your field of interest can probably provide cassettes or refer you to a source. A good example is the American Institute of Architects, which has a number of cassettes available, primarily with one topic per tape—"Construction Contracts" ($8.50), "Housing Systems" (with slides, $19), "Housing for the Elderly" (with a bibliography, $9.50), "Building Evaluation" (with booklet, $17). Perhaps the most interesting offering listed is "RAP . . . Review of Architectural Periodicals," described as a "monthly review of over fifty journals, news releases, newsletters, and other sources relevant to your practice. For maximum time effectiveness, hear the latest trends, developments, ideas, and forecasts in architecture while driving or doing routine jobs." A subscription, twelve cassettes, costs seventy-three dollars.

Major Sources for Instructional Audio Tape Cassettes

Canadian Broadcasting Company
Learning Systems
P.O. Box 500, Terminal A
Toronto, Canada

Interviews and documentaries on current social and cultural issues

The Cassette Curriculum
Everett/Edwards, Inc.
P.O. Box 1060
Deland, Florida 32720

A broad range of instructional tapes

Center for Cassette Studies
University Microfilms
300 N. Zeeb Road
Ann Arbor, Michigan 48106

Twenty-three subject areas covered

The Great Atlantic Radio
  Conspiracy
2743 Maryland Avenue
Baltimore, Maryland 21218

"Movement" tapes on sexism, art, politics, media, health, etc., from a radical point of view

The Living Library
P.O. Box 5405
Linden Hill Station
Flushing, New York 11354

Social change in education, ecology, and politics

Meditapes
Thomas More Association
180 N. Wabash Avenue
Chicago, Illinois 60601

Catholic-oriented but dealing with topics of broad interest: "The Right to Life," "The Occult," "Are You a Racist?" etc.

The Pacifica Foundation
2217 Shattuck Avenue
Berkeley, California 94704

Tapes of programs broadcast on the foundation's several listener-supported stations around the country

Tape Rental Library, Inc.
P.O. Box 2107
S. Vineland, New Jersey 08360

Business orientation, management seminars, sales courses

University Extension	Credit courses in academic
University of California	subjects
San Diego, California 92037	
Voice Over Books	Edited readings of current
P.O. Box 75	best-selling books
Old Chelsea Station	
New York, New York 10011	

REFERENCE BOOKS: FINDING CLUES TO PRACTICALLY ANYTHING

Reference books are the joy of some learners. There are a host of them—digests, directories, catalogs, indexes, bibliographies—ranging from the *Readers' Guide to Periodical Literature* and *Thomas' Register of American Manufacturers* to the *Negro Handbook* and the *Congressional Directory*. Some people delight not only in using those they know but also enjoy finding new ones. A friend of mine some years ago was quite awed that there was an *Obituary Index* compiled by the New York *Times*. To her surprise she found herself using it not much later when she was searching for information on a little-known author, dead some five years.

It certainly isn't necessary to identify at once or to memorize all the reference books that you may want to explore, for there are several reference books on reference books. My favorite, which I highly recommend, is *Reference Books: A Brief Guide*, compiled by Mary N. Barton and Marion V. Bell (Enoch Pratt Free Library, $1.25). It is a 158-page annotated listing of several hundred reference books, both of a general and of a specialized nature, in fields such as history, biology, business, economics, folklore, and mythology. The number of really good reference books listed in that "brief guide" and the several other guides is so large that there is not sufficient room here to give anything but a sampling.

Not surprisingly some of the best reference works are also

the best-known and most popular. The *New York Times Index*, easily available at most libraries, is a thorough and comprehensive guide to the extensive news coverage of the *Times*, past and present. Even if you are tracking down an obscure family murder of long ago, as a friend of mine did recently (knowing, incidentally, only the approximate year and the first names of the murderer and his victim), the *Index* can give you the date you need, and you can find your story. The *Index* covers a wide miscellany of topics, issues, and incidents (including, in fact, Murders), such as government activity, international affairs, urban development, arson, child abuse, judicial action, and gardening. It is easy to use, with an array of subject headings and concise but definitive abstracts of major news stories and abbreviated abstracts of lesser stories. The *Index* can, of course, point you to newspapers other than the *Times*. All you need is the date. A story about a flood in Minnesota may well be a *Times* item. But local coverage would probably be fuller.

We're all familiar with encyclopedias, almanacs, and books on Who's Who. They can provide accurate, quick facts about dates, places, happenings, people. Then there is the *Reader's Guide to Periodical Literature*, a well-used index of many general and non-technical magazines, though not of all. *Books in Print*, as its title suggests, is a catalog of books currently available from U.S. publishers. Books are listed by author and by title and, in a companion volume, *Subject Guide to Books in Print*, by subject. Both usually are available for reference in bookshops. *Paperbound Books in Print* lists some 90,000 entries by author, title, and subject.

Book Review Digest will lead you to reviews in newspapers and magazines written as long ago as 1905. If you want to find out how good a book is before you read it, the *Digest* will abstract for you the views of the book's reviewers. You can, of course, go to the source of the complete review to get the full version. Or use the *Digest* to compare your reactions to a book you have already read to see how they relate, particularly if you feel that you may have missed the point the writer was making. After all, it's reassuring to know when others agree that a writer may have failed to tell you enough.

Thomas' Register of American Manufacturers is a handy guide to finding out who manufactures what. If you want to find out who manufactures beer, soap, pencils, or thumbtacks, the *Register* lists each product separately.

As a hint to the variety of reference books, I list the *Encyclopaedia of Superstition*. It records more than two thousand superstitions of Britain, with explanatory and historical notes.

A final entry here is more a handbook than a reference book. It is *Finding Facts Fast* (Morrow Paperback Editions, $2.45) by Alden Todd. One of the points Todd makes in his really successful how-to book is that some of us would like to get the answers to our research questions more quickly than the university scholar. He also tells us that for our research we need not rely exclusively on books. He suggests we try public relations firms, trade associations, and foreign embassies. He suggests that a researcher can borrow techniques not only from the librarian and scholar but also from investigative reporters and detectives. "With practice any intelligent person can master the research methods appropriate to his immediate purpose or line of work, without memorizing things that he can look up easily."

NEW ROUTES TO YOUR DIPLOMA

Colleges and universities are currently reaching out to free learners with programs that provide various new opportunities for degrees. You can:

• Complete the class work required for a degree at convenient times—such as in the evening, on weekends, or during the summer—and in your own community rather than coming to the campus.

- Develop a personal plan of study through independent reading and field work related to your occupation, which will earn you a diploma.
- Obtain credits for prior learning, whether in a classroom or on your own.*
- Take courses via television or through a combination of televised instruction, correspondence study, and other media.
- Earn a degree solely by examination.

To find such opportunities in your community, scan the newspapers for ads featuring come-ons like "You're Closer Than You Think to a College Degree," "Weekend College," "External Degree," "University Without Walls," "TV College," or "Lifelong Learning."

I have written two booklets on these kinds of programs. *Higher/Wider Education* is available free from the Office of Reports, The Ford Foundation, 320 East 43rd Street, New York, New York 10017. *New Paths to Learning* can be obtained at most libraries or from the Public Affairs Committee, 381 Park Avenue S., New York, New York 10016, for the nominal price of fifty cents.

These booklets cover such programs as the following:

- The University Without Walls is a national network of programs at twenty-seven colleges and universities. In it students are offered alternative ways to obtain degrees through individually planned programs based largely on off-campus learning and independent study.
- Empire State College, an innovative unit of the vast State University of New York, replaces classroom instruction with learning contracts and teachers with "mentors" who work with students individually.
- The Regents (New York) External Degree Program enables people who believe they have learned on their own what is taught in college courses to show what they know by examination and thereby earn a degree. It is available to learners throughout the country.

* You can obtain such credits without being enrolled in such a program. See the "Show What You Know" section.

• The University of Mid-America, a regional effort, spans the states of Iowa, Kansas, Missouri, and Nebraska to bring higher learning to everyone who wants it, via television, other media, and academic support services.

Much as I applaud these new opportunities for higher education, I must conclude with a note of warning. There is a danger here for free learners. It is all too easy to become enslaved by one of these programs—to find that what started as a useful *means* to obtaining credits and a degree for what you really want to learn becomes instead a dominating and distracting compulsion to meet the requirements of the program.

Already I have seen such corruption occurring. In some "contract learning" programs students are pressured into selecting "goals" for their learning on the basis of what they can easily accomplish in order to earn credits, rather than being encouraged to take the risks which real learning always involves.

Perhaps the greatest danger in this field is the misguided movement which John Ohliger, a brilliant radical critic of the adult education establishment though himself a distinguished scholar in the field, calls "mandatory adult education." By this phrase he means the movement to make continuing education compulsory, like schooling. He points to the emerging regulations requiring professionals of various kinds—doctors and lawyers, for instance—to take further courses in their field to retain their licenses. Or the imposition of mandatory training on welfare recipients.

Ohliger isn't against continued learning. It is a passion of his life. But he rightly opposes compulsory courses as the way to get people to learn and grow. He believes, and I agree, that such a system is more likely to benefit the educators who give the courses than the professionals or the general public.

Unfortunately, colleges hungry for tuition dollars are all too ready to manipulate students this way. To some of them,

Some Sourcebooks on New Degree Programs

This Way Out: A Guide to Alternatives to Traditional Education in the U.S., Europe, and the 3rd World, John Coyne and Tom Hebert, Dutton, New York.

College Learning, Anytime, Anywhere, Ewald Nyquist, Jack Arbolino, and Gene Hawes, Harcourt Brace Jovanovich, New York.

The New York Times Guide to Continuing Education in America, Quadrangle Books, New York.

The Regnery/Cowles CLEP Book, Cowles, New York.

Guide to Alternative Colleges and Universities, Wayne Blaze, *et al.,* Beacon, Boston.

College Degrees by Mail: A Comprehensive Guide to Degree Programs, John Bear, Drawer H., Littleriver, California 95456

Two good sources of information about innovative programs in higher education:

    Office of New Degree Programs
    College Entrance Examination Board
    888 Seventh Avenue
    New York, New York 10019
    (John Valley, Director)

    NEXUS
    c/o American Association for Higher Education
    1 Dupont Circle
    Washington, D.C. 20036
    (Jane Lichtman, Director)

people who want to learn are of interest mainly as paying clients. Watch out for programs which seem more intent on running you through an expensive regimen to "earn" your credits than in being helpful to you in pursuing your learning. Remember that your goal is to grow, not merely to matriculate.

EDUCATIONAL BROKERS

So numerous have these new degree programs become that a new kind of educational professional—one who can be extremely helpful to free learners—has emerged in the last year or so to help individuals find the right programs. The "educational broker" is an individual or agency (usually non-profit) that matches you and your needs with the programs, materials, and other resources available in your field of interest. The educational broker can help you pinpoint what you want to learn and how you want to learn it, brief you on the different ways you can accomplish your goals, help you plan your program and overcome any problems that arise in the process.

The leading example of the educational broker is the Regional Learning Service of Central New York. One of many similar organizations in the country, this non-profit organization helps residents of a five-county area who want to obtain a high school or college diploma, to change careers, or to learn simply for the joy of it. The service is voluntary, low cost, flexible, and personal. Through learning consultants, an individual, either by himself or as one of a small group, can get sensitive and informed advice on formulating goals, planning or finding a program, and following through. All this is available to anyone over sixteen years old who wants help about further education or career development. The cost is only fifteen dollars for the first three months and ten dollars more to renew.

Not a school or college itself, the Regional Learning Service does not teach or award degrees. "We're basically just matchmakers," says Fran Macy, director and one of the chief architects of both the RLS and the whole idea of educational brokerage. "At our right hand are the adults in this community who want and need further education and help in pursuing their occupational and professional goals. At our left hand is the vast and complex array of educational programs, old and new: not just private and public colleges and universities, but correspondence study, offerings by unions, churches, and other voluntary agencies and state and federal government programs.

"It's a dazzling array of options—but a confusing one for the new adult learner, if he knows about them at all. Our job is to learn enough about the learner and help him learn enough about himself and these options to make the best match. Our tools may include diagnostic testing, career planning, and educational counseling. We can assess what the client already knows and help him get credit for that out-of-school learning. Then, when and if he chooses to return to a formal educational program, we can help him make the choice, get in, and get through."

To play the role honestly and effectively, it is important that the educational broker or learning consultant be independent of any educational institution in which the learner might enroll. Counselors employed by colleges might well see their institutions' offerings as what the learner needs, especially in these days when most institutions of higher education are frankly hungry for warm bodies. The educational broker, on the other hand, maintains a disinterested but comprehensive awareness of the entire range of options that might serve different learners' needs.

"Client advocacy means placing learners' needs and interests above those of institutions," insists Macy. "We're willing and often able to intervene in a client's behalf to cut through red tape, and sometimes to incite broader changes in institutional policies that are hampering many learners:

inflexible scheduling, rigid rules about entrance requirements. It's our independent status that enables us to do
this. No professor or administrator, no matter how student-
oriented he may be, can act so readily as advocates for students' interests against 'the system' in his own institution.
We can, and do.'"

Some Major Educational Brokers Around the Country

EASTERN PROGRAMS

Capital Higher Education Service
275 Windsor Street
Hartford, Connecticut 06120
(203) 527-5261

Career Counseling Service
Ocean State Training Center
  Building 808
Quonset Point, Rhode Island
  02819
(401) 294-2150

Community College of Vermont
P.O. Box 81
Montpelier, Vermont 05602
(802) 828-2401

Educational Opportunity Center
  Program
Executive Office of Educational
  Affairs
18 Tremont Street
Boston, Massachusetts 02149
(617) 727-7785

Hudson Community College
  Commission
26 Journal Square
Jersey City, New Jersey 07306
(201) 656-2020

New Jersey Education Consortium
228 Alexander Street
Princeton, New Jersey 08540
(609) 921-2021

Pennsylvania Adult Counseling
  Program
Department of Education
Box 911
Harrisburg, Pennsylvania 17126
(717) 787-9602

Regional Continuing Education
  for Women Program
Temple University
Broad and Montgomery
Philadelphia, Pennsylvania 19122
(215) 787-7602

Regional Learning Service of
  Central New York
405 Oak Street
Syracuse, New York 13203
(315) 477-8430

Thomas A. Edison College
1750 North Olden Avenue
Trenton, New Jersey 08638
(609) 292-8092

Women's Inner-City Education
Resource Service Center
90 Warren Street
Roxbury, Massachusetts 02119
(617) 440-9150

SOUTHERN AND MIDWESTERN
PROGRAMS

Center for Open Learning
Alabama Consortium for the
Development of Higher
Education
306 N. Main
Demopolis, Alabama 36736
(205) 289-0177

Community-Based Counseling
for Adults
Office of Student Services
University of Wisconsin-Extension
Lake Street
Madison, Wisconsin 53706
(608) 263-2055

Greater Cleveland External
Degree Service
Cleveland Public Library
325 Superior Avenue NE.
Cleveland, Ohio 44114
(216) 621-5557

School for New Learning
DePaul University
23 East Jackson Boulevard
Chicago, Illinois 60604
(312) 939-3525 Ext. 258

WESTERN PROGRAMS

Okanogan County Education
Service
Wenatchee Valley College
Box 2058
Omak, Washington 98841
(509) 826-4901

This listing of educational brokering programs and related agencies concerned with providing information and counseling for adult learners was compiled by the National Center for Educational Brokering.

"SHOW WHAT YOU KNOW"—
OBTAINING CREDIT FOR FREE LEARNING

Obtaining credit for what you've learned on your own is one advantage of the New Degree programs just described. But you can obtain such credit without even being enrolled in such a program.

"Show What You Know" might be the motto of these ways to earn college credit with the least possible cost or hassle.

New York State has pioneered in developing these op- portunities by using the best tests that already exist and in- venting some of its own. Fortunately, the state makes most of these services available to people all over the country, so as you read what follows don't despair if you live west of the Hudson. You can benefit from almost all of the New York State initiatives. Moreover, since many states are start- ing their own programs, there's a good chance that by the time you read these lines there may be home-grown op- portunities like New York's for you to use.

Here's a brief run-down of the major ways to have your learning given the imprimatur:

- *CLEP (College Level Examination Program)*. A national pro- gram of credit-by-examination sponsored by the College Ex- amination Board. The fee is twenty dollars for one exam, thirty dollars for two, forty for three to five. More than a thousand colleges and universities in the country award credit; they are listed in publications available from CLEP. CLEP just gives you your score. It's up to you to find a college that accepts the score for credit, and you should shop around to get the best deal.
- *CPE (College Proficiency Examinations)*. A New York State program, much like CLEP, but supplemented with added ex- ams in fields not covered by CLEP, such as philosophy of education, music, Shakespeare, criminal justice, health educa- tion, typing. The New York State Education Department makes these tests available throughout the country, through the Ameri- can College Testing Program (ACT), and awards its own college credits for them *if* you're enrolled in the Regents Ex- ternal Degree Program. Otherwise, as above, you have to arrange for your credits with a cooperative college.
- *Regents External Degree Examinations (New York State)*. The RED differs from CLEP and CPE in that the tests do *not* cover areas of knowledge comparable to some college course but rather test your level of preparation in such specialties as nursing, business, or foreign languages. Like the CPE, they are available to non–New Yorkers through ACT.
- *Special Assessment Examination Program of RED*. Even if you

have an unusual skill or proficiency for which no testing exists, you can get one custom made under this program. These examinations may be oral, written, or performance tests, or the evaluation of portfolios of artistic or literary accomplishments, or a combination. Credit earned under this program can be applied to all independent study programs. The amount of credit granted in a Special Assessment Examination, and the cost, will vary according to the learning being evaluated. You should expect to pay approximately $200 to $250 for each Special Assessment.

- *The Regents Credit Bank.* A college-level evaluation and transcript service, the Credit Bank will evaluate scores earned on proficiency tests such as CLEP, CPE, those given by the United States Armed Forces Institute, and the Regents External Degree examinations. It will also assess courses taken in the military service, and courses offered by businesses such as General Electric, Xerox, American Institute of Banking, as well as college courses taken on campus or by correspondence from accredited institutions. The results are recorded on official transcripts and forwarded to any person, agency, or educational institution upon your request. The Credit Bank enables you to consolidate your academic records for employment or educational purposes. It is designed for persons *not* enrolled in the External Degree program, since these services are already provided to those pursuing a Regents External Degree. A fee of fifty dollars will open a Credit Bank record for two years, during which an unlimited number of evaluations will be provided.

- *The Office on Non-Collegiate Sponsored Instruction.* This office evaluates courses offered by organizations whose primary focus is not education—that is, private industry, professional associations, labor unions, voluntary associations, and government agencies. After review of programs and courses, the New York State Education Department recommends how much credit to award for satisfactory completion by a student. As in the case of CLEP and CPE, a college must accept the recommended credit established for a course before the student who has completed the course can receive academic credit toward a degree.

For Information on Testing Programs

College-Level Examination
  Program
P.O. Box 1824
Princeton, New Jersey 08540

New York College Proficiency
  Examinations
State Education Department
Room 1913, 99 Washington
  Avenue
Albany, New York 12230

Regents External Degree
  Examinations
State Education Department
Room 1913, 99 Washington
  Avenue
Albany, New York 12230

For information about New York
examinations administered outside
New York State:
American College Testing
  Program
P.O. Box 168
Iowa City, Iowa 52240

Chapter 6 / FREE LEARNERS, FREE PEOPLE

Liberty without learning is always in peril;
learning without liberty is always in vain.
—JOHN F. KENNEDY

If this book has started you on fresh adventures in self-development, it has achieved its purpose. But there's a larger dimension to free learning than individual growth. Lifelong learning has a social significance too.

Free learners are fulfilling the highest goal that educators themselves proclaim for formal schooling. Helping students "learn how to learn," launching them on trajectories of lifelong self-education—this is the ostensible goal of virtually every school and college in the country. Look at the official purposes of your own community's public schools, or the opening pages of any college catalog. All educators agree in principle with Arnold Toynbee's dictum: "Intellectual independence at the earliest possible age should be the objective of education. . . . The initiative should be transferred to the student himself at the earliest practicable stage. . . . The educational ladder should hoist the climber up from the child's passive role to the adult's active one."

So by taking command of their own education, free learners achieve the true "commencement"—the end of being taught what "everybody must know" and the beginning of teaching oneself whatever each person as an individual most needs to discover.

This larger social value of free learning transcends the

particular things learned. It is a lever for life-change. Free learning sparks in people what Professor Benjamin DeMott calls a "reconfirmation of the energies of individuality, the power to choose a direction for oneself and to commit one's labor and capital to it as a free and vital being."

That is a rare feeling in our society; perhaps the human condition makes it a precarious achievement in *any* society. But the shaping of our own minds is, as the Stoics taught, the one area where we have the best chance to exercise autonomy. Certainly it is the place to start.

The point is well made by the distinguished American historian Howard Mumford Jones. Glossing the Declaration's affirmation of man's right to "life, liberty, and the pursuit of happiness," he points out that "the only durable meaning of 'life' in this context is one's inner life, the only use of 'liberty' is long-run freedom to enrich that inner life, and the only possible meaning of happiness lies in some less transient satisfaction than eating and drinking, getting and spending, and being amused."

The free learner has a public aspect too—as the mainstay of a democratic society. For free learning expresses the faith that people can make their own appraisals of what they need and want, that they can take responsibility for their own development, and that a nation can be run on the basis of their collective judgment.

This faith is basic to the American experiment in self-government. From the beginnings and throughout our history, our national ideal has been the intellectually self-reliant individual.

The Founding Fathers had a revolutionary idea of how Americans could best learn and grow. In their view, schools and colleges had only a subordinate part to play in education. They did not make the mistake, as we often do, of confusing schooling with education. And needless to say they did not make the even worse mistake of judging people by their diplomas.

Rather, our revolutionary forebears believed that *real*

learning was personal and lifelong. It flowed from each individual's constant quest to become all that he or she is capable of being. "Jefferson was a great believer in schooling," points out educational historian Lawrence Cremin, "but it never occurred to him that schooling would be the chief educational influence on the young. Schooling might provide technical skills and basic knowledge, but it was the press and participation in politics that really educated the citizenry."

One can trace this theme throughout American history: in the potent tradition of self-education stretching from Ben Franklin and Abraham Lincoln through Thomas Edison and Henry Ford down to Eric Hoffer and Malcolm X in our own day; in the invention of ingenious means of "diffusing knowledge" like the Lyceums and Chautauquas; in the flowering of public libraries and the growth of newspapers and magazines; and above all in the great liberation movements which taught us the truth about ourselves—the Revolution itself, abolitionism, and most recently the struggles of blacks, women, and others. (I have explored this tradition of free learning in American culture in "A Nation of Learners," the title essay in a volume of American Education Bicentennial Essays available from the U.S. Office of Education, Washington, D.C.)

Free learning has always found a passionate voice among radical critics: Tom Paine, Thoreau, and Paul Goodman all exalted the free learner over the merely school-taught, who all too often has only absorbed what the powers that be want him to know. Here in America, Emerson wrote in the essay which declared this nation's cultural independence from the old country, the scholar should simply be Man Thinking.

Our politics has been premised on the notion that each of us can function, in however modest a degree, as a free-thinking citizen, an independent center of understanding, judgment, and action. Our commitment to free speech and a free press springs from this conviction—that the best way to find the truth is for the full range of ideas and information to be openly debated by the citizenry. Such a "market place of ideas" makes no sense if people cannot cope with information and ideas, probe from meanings, come to judgments, and, perhaps, wisdom—in short, keep on learning.

It is widely acknowledged that we live today in a society whose ubiquitous media and conformist pressures distract us from our deepest needs. How then can we lift ourselves —and the society—to a more humane level? The answer lies in the capacity of individuals to conceive finer possibilities of learning and growth, and then to share their adventure and their discoveries with the rest of us. Free learners constitute an independent sector of our intellectual life out of which arise many of the new insights we need.

I have never seen this put better than in a statement by the critic and novelist Philip Wylie shortly before he died. He was trying to imagine what capacities we would have to develop to cope with the world of future shock. "If there are any Americans with an education sufficient for useful criticism and constructive proposals," he wrote, "one fact about them will be sure: they will be self-educated. . . . They will be people who learned how to learn and to want to learn—people who did not stop learning when they received their degree or degrees—people who developed a means of evaluation of all knowledge in order to determine what they had to understand for useful thought—people who, then, knew what they did not know and learned that if necessary."

Since free learning generates these social benefits, it deserves the support of the society quite as much as institutionalized education. Traditionally, virtually all the public support for education has gone to schools and colleges, and to students enrolled in them. It is time to balance this support of formal instruction with support for free learning.

I would like to see funds for lifelong learning go not just to existing institutions but to individual learners to use in the ways they see fit. Why not grants, scholarships, vouchers, sabbaticals, support facilities, encouragement, and recognition for people of all ages who are ready, willing, and able to learn?

We have poured billions of dollars into our present highly structured instructional bureaucracies. But only recently have we begun to experiment with supporting learning resources, open to all, which truly place themselves at the disposal of learners. "Why does the government regard sending citizens to school or even to college as so important that the opportunity should be furnished free by the state," asked historian James Flexner, apropos the fiscal crisis of New York City's famed Public Library, "and yet allow libraries to languish? ... Does education mean only taking courses? Surely self-education, once universally recognized as basic to the American spirit, remains basic to all learning."

I would like to see an upsurge in offerings and options for learners through the burgeoning of all kinds of fresh initiatives: learning exchanges, free universities, study and action groups, social change alliances, special interest networks, small publications and newsletters, open access media, catalogs, expanded library services. Here too public subventions would be most welcome.

But none of this will happen automatically. Such changes will occur only if a substantial constituency takes shape— people pressing their institutions and their government officials to support a more open, various, flexible, and individualized system of learning opportunities. Without such pressure, the limited funds available for education will tend to flow in the old, well-established channels.

Yet those channels—conventional college and university degree programs—do not have sufficiently diverse offerings to meet the needs of enough people. Rather than make adult learning opportunities available to everyone on a fair and inviting basis, they always end up providing additional education for those who need it least—the already well educated, the well-to-do, the successful. "Blacks, the poor and the undereducated are substantially underrepresented among adult learners," Edward Rosenthal of Rutgers University has shown. "The 'lifelong learning' boom has primarily benefited those who have privilege." Growth in adult education has only reinforced the educational gaps between black and white, poor and rich, the unschooled and the schooled.

But if a strong constituency for a truly open system of adult learning opportunities does develop, the future favors free learners. There is talk in Washington of funding lifelong learning through "entitlement"—scholarships which could be used at any point in one's life to pay for educational experiences, rather than only when one is of college age. New services such as learner's advisers in libraries and educational brokers are emerging to meet the needs of free learners. Courses are increasingly available over television, in newspapers, by correspondence, on cassettes, providing an endless supply of materials and resources to suit every taste and learning style.

New technology is coming that will be useful to free learners, such as reasonably priced home videotape players and recordings which can be used the way we now use long-playing phonograph records. There will be more and better courses broadcast over TV and radio, and cheaper telephone service providing access to computers for information and problem solving. These will all be welcome, of course. But frankly I don't think such technological innovations will make the decisive difference for free learning. What is essential is the desire to learn and grow. No new electronic wonders will transform apathetic individuals into self-change artists. But given the will to learn, each free learner will naturally make use of whatever new resources and media come along.

Institutions can help too. Colleges, which once spurned adult students, are, as we have seen, now bending over backwards to welcome free learners back to the campus, and, more important, offering them help in learning on their own terms. Employers are less and less interested in mere credentials, more and more in what "competencies"—actual knowledge, understanding, and skills—applicants have.

Most important of all, we Americans as individuals seem to be developing a fresh hunger for experience, for growth, for personal cultivation. Men and women of all ages today feel the urge to seek more in life—to shape a larger self. That quest I call lifelong learning.

Chapter 7

THE LIFELONG LEARNER'S BASIC BOOKSHELF

> *I honestly think I could not manage to stay centered without the comforting and frequent hours I spend with the right kind of books.*
> —IRV THOMAS

On the Spirit of Lifelong Learning

Emerson's "Self-Reliance" and "The American Scholar." In these two essays Emerson laid the foundation for the American tradition of independent thought. "There is a time in every man's education," he wrote in "Self-Reliance," "when he arrives at the conviction that envy is ignorance; that imitation is suicide; that he must take himself for better or worse as his portion; that though the wide universe is full of good, no kernel of nourishing corn can come to him but through his toil bestowed on that part of ground which is given him to till." In "American Scholar," Emerson proclaimed that the native genius of our culture lies in its reliance on individual thinking unconstrained by tradition, convention, or academic authority.

Thoreau's *Walden* and "Life Without Principle." "Let nothing come between you and the light." Thoreau provided personal testimony to the Emersonian ideal. These two works deal largely with the why and how of intellectual autonomy. The man who "traveled far in Concord" learned from everything: nature, friends, books, and above all through making his utterly personal evaluation of them all.

171

Benjamin Franklin's *Autobiography.* A treatise on self-education from a far different point of view than Emerson's and Thoreau's, one to my mind less congenial to our own style. But Franklin devised some marvelous principles and tricks of free learning, including what we now call behavior modification. And he saw how fruitfully people could join together for learning in clubs, discussion groups, libraries, and schools rightly run.

Cyril O. Houle *The Inquiring Mind,* University of Wisconsin Press, 1961.* An urbane and stimulating study of "the adult who continues to learn" mainly through taking adult education courses but also independently. If you're curious about why you really want to learn, this book will enlighten you about your motives and those of others you will meet along the way. Professor Houle of the University of Chicago is perhaps the wisest and certainly the most cultivated scholar in the field of adult education. "The desire to learn, like every other human characteristic, is not shared equally by everyone," his book begins. "But in a world which sometimes seems to stress the pleasures of ignorance, some men and women seek the rewards of knowledge. . . . The desire to learn seems, in fact, to pervade their existence. They approach life with an air of openness and an inquiring mind."

Ernest Lindeman, *The Meaning of Adult Education,* Harvest House (Montreal), 1961.* Lindeman's formal education began at the age of twenty-one, after he had earned his way in the world since the age of nine in the shipbuilding trade, participating in strikes and working in factories. Eventually he became a distinguished teacher of sociology as well as philosophy and earned the accolade of "father of adult education in the United States." Among his accomplishments was the initiation of the Mentor series of classic reprints, one of the most distinguished quality paperback

* An asterisk in this section indicates paperback edition.

lines ever produced. His book is a spirited and eloquent rationale for adult learning as an autonomous realm of education, quite distinct from the schooling of children. This education—which we have called free learning—continues throughout life, is rooted in the situations and circumstances of life rather than in academic subjects, and is shaped by and for the individual. Lindeman shows how such learning is needed for the fulfillment of our potentialities for creativity, freedom, power, and intelligent living.

James R. Kidd, *How Adults Learn,* Association Press, 1959. A classic non-technical treatment of the adult learning process, oriented toward adult educators but containing, particularly in the initial chapters ("Learning Throughout Life," "The Adult Learner"), much material of use to free learners. Professor Kidd summarizes the findings which lie behind the principles I have affirmed in the opening chapter of this book. As he says, one who asserts such principles "may be accused of overoptimism." But what he presents about the capacity of adults is neither sentimentality nor romanticism; it is based on observed performance under exacting conditions. "More and more, as objective evidence comes in, it becomes clearer that man has only begun to use the resources of his mind and being. ... All human beings can be aided to become increasingly self-reliant and autonomous."

Michael Rossman, *On Learning and Social Change,* Random House, 1972. Rossman, whose perceptive account of his self-education in music will be recalled from the text, was a leader of the Free Speech movement on the Berkeley campus in the late 1960s and has emerged subsequently as an articulate spokesman for a less conspicuous but maturing counterculture. In this book he sees free learning occurring through the myriad enterprises of this counterculture: free universities, underground papers, radical caucuses within the major professions, learning exchanges, etc. "Our culture's central failure is its inability to help its people and itself to learn how to learn," he writes, and then sketches the characteristics of what he calls the "self-directed learner, who is able to change his behavior to meet his needs and thus has learned how to learn. What he does is *create knowledge.*"

Ivan Illich, *Deschooling Society,* Harrow Books, Harper & Row, 1972.* This is a highly provocative attack on formal education as antithetical to genuine learning. "I see human perfection in the progressive elimination of the institutional intermediary between man and the truth he wants to learn."

John Gardner, *Self-Renewal,* Harper & Row, 1963.* "Exploration of the full range of his own potentialities is not something that the self-renewing man leaves to the chances of life," argues Gardner. "It is something he pursues systematically, or at least avidly, to the end of his days." Gardner's treatment is particularly useful because it stresses the need for social and organizational reform if individuals are to be liberated to pursue this ideal of self-fulfillment.

John Holt, *Instead of Education: Ways to Help People Do Things Better,* Dutton, 1976. Taking a more radical and polemical position than I do, Holt urges that the *only* learning is learning by doing. But his evocation of the learning life, and his practical suggestions for turning our society into one that conduces to human growth, are supportive and often brilliant.

On the Methods of Free Learning

John Coyne and Tom Hebert, "Independent Study," in *This Way Out,* Dutton, 1972. The first hundred pages of Coyne and Hebert's catalog constitute a brisk, brash, often helpful but occasionally too flip treatise on learning on your own. Taken with a grain of salt, it's stimulating medicine for anyone who has apprehensions about the possibilities of self-education.

Cyril Houle, *Continuing Your Education,* McGraw-Hill, 1964. Houle gives common-sense advice on such subjects as how to make yourself a time and place to learn, how to think about your further education, and on study methods.

Allen Tough, *The Adult's Learning Projects*, Ontario Institute for Studies in Education, 1971.* Based on in-depth interviews with people about their self-teaching, this unique study goes into detail about typical approaches, problems, techniques, and feelings.

Malcolm Knowles, *Self-Directed Learning: A Guide for Learners and Teachers*, Association Press, 1975.* A manual on the planning and conduct of learning projects as a form of individualized higher education. Too stiffly academic in approach for the freewheeling learning style which I have advocated, but well-worth having on hand as a guide to the best that has been devised by the professors to help people learn on their own.

Gail Sheehy, *Passages: Predictable Crises of Adult Life*, Dutton, 1976. This popular exposition of recent studies shows that adults, like children, pass through discernible stages of development. Recognizing these typical crisis periods in our own lives, we can better manage them so that they become periods of learning and growth rather than merely scaring and scarring us.

Ari Kiev, *A Strategy for Daily Living*, Free Press (Macmillan), 1973. Since self-development through learning is a basic strategy for successful living, virtually any first-rate self-help book will include it. I've listed this one here to represent the genre. Kiev's chapter on "Modification of Behavior" asks, "When was the last time you applied your intellect to a new project designed to elevate your self-concept by overcoming habitual patterns of thought?" By staying in good condition psychologically, Kiev argues, "you can train yourself to master the stress of crises."

John C. Crystal and Richard N. Bolles, *Where Do I Go from Here with My Life?* Seabury, 1974.* The best of the new genre of "Life/Work Planning" systems for exploring your potentialities and strengths, setting personal goals, and managing your life to get what you want and become what you aspire to be. Useful for putting the kind of self-educational planning which I have advocated in a broader perspective.

Alan Lakein, *How to Get Control of Your Time and Your Life*, Signet, 1973.* Here is a good quick course in rational goal setting and time management. "I try to put more thinking into what people do," explains the author. "So please don't call me an efficiency expert. I'm an 'effectiveness expert.' Effectiveness means selecting the best task to do from all the possibilities available and then doing it the best way. Making the right choices about how you'll use your time is more important than doing efficiently whatever job happens to be around."

Arnold Bennett, *How to Live on 24 Hours a Day*, Cornerstone Library, 1975.* Not, as its title implies, a book about the management of time in everyday affairs, but a manual for opening space in one's life for learning, "exceeding one's programme" as Bennett calls it. His conception of learning transcends the literary and artistic: "The most important of all perceptions is the continual perception of cause and effect—in other words, the perception of the course of evolution. When one has thoroughly got imbued into one's head the leading truth that nothing happens without a cause, one grows not only large-minded but large-hearted."

C. A. Mace, *The Psychology of Study*, Pelican, 1968.* The best short book on how our minds work, and how we can best make them work, when set to the task of conventional kinds of learning.

Jacques Barzun and Henry Graff, *The Modern Researcher*, Harcourt Brace Jovanovich, 1974. This is an excellent handbook on general methods of finding out things from books and other written documents, based on the methods of the historian but generalized into an approach to library research. Sound and nicely written, but too narrowly focused on traditional modes of learning.

Alden Todd, *Finding Facts Fast*, William Morrow, 1972.*

A very succinct and handy volume showing how to use every tool of the library, many of which most people have never heard of. And it includes some even more enterprising methods like "Finding the Person Who Knows," or getting help from your congressman.

C. Wright Mills, "On Intellectual Craftsmanship," in *The Sociological Imagination*, Evergreen Books, 1961.* An invigorating short treatise on how to become your own social scientist, by one of the best professional ones. For Mills, an inquiring response to one's society—to those points at which "biography intersects with history"—is not an academic specialty but a part of the full life.

Carlos Castaneda, *The Teachings of Don Juan*, Ballantine, 1969.* The classic exploration of superrational ways of learning and growth. Essential to put into perspective our more familiar modes of knowing.

Peter Elbow, *Writing Without Teachers*, Oxford University Press, 1973.* Writing is—or should be—as much a part of learning as is reading. And almost everyone would like to write more and better, anyway. Here is a proven formula for growing into a better writer in the company of friends, without formal study or paying for a course or teacher.

Ira Progoff, *At a Journal Workshop*, Dialogue House Library, 1976. The authoritative guide to using an introspective journal for self-discovery and self-affirmation.

Tony Buzan, *Use Both Sides of Your Brain*, Dutton Paperback, 1976.* These innovative approaches to studying on your own include unconventional techniques for reading more efficiently, memorizing, problem solving, note taking, and writing. The basic philosophy of the book is congenial to free learners: "In traditional education information is given or 'taught' about the different areas of knowledge that surround the individual. The direction and flow is *from* the subject *to* the individual—he is simply given the information, and is expected to absorb, learn and remember as much as he possibly can. . . . In the new forms of education [these] emphases must be reversed. Instead of first teaching the individual facts about other things, we must first teach him facts about himself—facts about how he *can* learn, think, recall, create, and solve problems."

Some Accounts of Lifelong Learners in Action

Simone de Beauvoir, *Autobiography*, Warner Books, 1973.* An absorbing account of the maturation of a superb intelligence. Simone de Beauvoir has lived at the center of European intellectual, political, and cultural life, but she has also kept closely in touch with her personal processes of growing up and growing old, which all of us experience in much the same way. The result is both cosmopolitan and intimate.

Paul Goodman, *Five Years*, Vintage Books, Random House, 1969.* The daily diary of an intellect as powerful as de Beauvoir's, but isolated from other outstanding people during a period of frustration. Goodman wrote much of this book as a fiftyish self-confessed failure whose career and personal life had collapsed. Yet his mind thrived.

Cornelius Hirschberg, *The Priceless Gift*, Simon and Schuster, 1960. The not-very-successful New York salesman we meet in the text writes of the rich learning life he created for himself from the classics of Western literature.

Eric Hoffer, *Working and Thinking on the Waterfront*, Harper & Row, 1969. The longshoreman-writer's daily diary of a year of laboring and learning, showing how daily experience, reading, and the determination to make sense of the world give rise to insight.

Alfred Sloan, Jr., *My Years with General Motors*, Anchor Books, Doubleday, 1972.* A classic account of a top-level manager with a style open enough to learn, and thereby able to lead a major corporation through a treacherous economy.

Malcolm X, *Autobiography*, Grove Press, 1973.* The story of how a persecuted criminal came to recognize the power of his own mind and translate understanding into leadership.

Harold Lyon, *It's Me and I'm Here!* Delacorte Press, 1974. The subtitle says it well: "From West Point to Esalen: The Struggles of an Overachiever to Revitalize His Life Through the Human Potential Movement." Learning not from books but from intensive growth experiences.

Michael Rossman, *Learning Without a Teacher*, Phi Delta Kappa Fastback, 1974.* A brilliant evocation of the author's experiences with music—as a skill, as a paradigm of lifelong learning, and as a preparation for his life-style of political activism.

Lynn Caine, *Widow*, Bantam, 1975.* This is a stirring, eloquent, candid account of how Lynn Caine survived the death of a beloved spouse and learned the terrible things that had to be done to become "a different woman."

Mike Cherry, *On High Steel: The Education of an Ironworker*, Ballantine, 1975.* Complex skills and keen judgment are learned by doing, among men who "scarcely use words at all."

Jessamyn West, *Hide and Seek: A Continuing Journey*, Harcourt Brace Jovanovich, 1973. Learning is pursued through solitariness. The distinguished author spent three months alone in a trailer along a remote bank of the Colorado River, yet found that her keen sense of the present, and the past, made the time one of growth and sharpened self-understanding.

John Robben, *Coming to My Senses*, T. Y. Crowell, 1973. The mid-life emotional awakening of a suburban businessman, recorded in an intimate journal of frustration and growth.

Herbert Kohl, *Half the House*, Bantam, 1976.* "Is it possible to change oneself in midlife despite one's education and the practical pressures to survive?" A West Coast teacher-writer tackles this question through a memoir-reflection on his own struggles with self and society.

INDEX

academic credit, self-education and, 51
accredited schools, 93
activist groups, 89
"adjunct faculty," 141
adult(s)
    as learners, 58–61
    learning methods of, 17
adult education, 50–51
    "mandatory," 153
adulthood, personality and, 59
Adult Independent Learning Project, 98
Adult's Learning Projects, The (Tough), 175
AFL-CIO, 123
Aims of Education, The (Whitehead), 54–55
airliners, commercial, interest in, 100
Akiba, Rabbi, 71
Allen, Pamela, 111
Alliance Française, 92
Alternate Sources of Energy, 103
American Association of Retired Persons, 123
American Civil Liberties Union, 34
American College Testing Program, 159
American Dream, 30
American Education Bicentennial Essays, 165
American Institute of Architects, 147

American Institute of Banking, 160
American Red Cross, 123
American Society of Civil Engineers, 54
American Youth Hostel, 92
Andrus, Barbara, 42–48, 83
Anstett, Robert, 45
Apprenticeship Information Center, 122
apprenticeships, 122–23
Aquinas, St. Thomas, 25
Arbolino, Jack, 154
Aristotle, 13
art centers, learning through, 88
arts, education in, 119–21
Ascent of Man, The (Bronowski), 113
Asiatic history, 25
Association of Junior Leagues, 123
At a Journal Workshop (Progoff), 177
Atlantic, early crossings of, 40
Autobiography (de Beauvoir), 178
Autobiography (Franklin), 172
Autobiography (Malcolm X), 178
"auto-didactical" education, 20
    see also self-education
avocational academics, 40

Bach, Johann Sebastian, 32
Bacon, Sir Francis, 25

181